YOU CAN TEACH YOURSELF
PIANO

By Matt Dennis

Preface

You Can Teach Yourself Piano is a new concept in piano literature. Upon completion of this method, the student will be fully equipped to handle the demands of modern music. In addition, the student will receive the intangible assets of ear development and taste in contemporary sounds.

Dedication

To my wife, Ginny Maxey, for her encouragement and understanding
&
to all those who love the better sounds in music and who aspire to learn to play the piano for pleasure, in a reasonably short time, and *enjoy* the learning process.
Matt Dennis

A stereo cassette tape of the music in this book is now available. The publisher strongly recommends the use of this cassette tape along with the text to insure accuracy of interpretation and ease in learning.

TABLE OF CONTENTS

BEGINNING FUNDAMENTALS

As you sit at the **PIANO** . . . directly in front of you is the **MIDDLE** section of

THE PIANO KEYBOARD

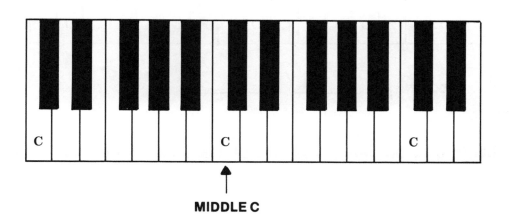

MIDDLE C

The complete **PIANO KEYBOARD** is made up of a series of **BLACK** and **WHITE KEYS,** left to right, from bottom to top. The **BLACK KEYS** are in alternate groups of **TWO** and **THREE.** The **WHITE KEYS** have the names of

THE SEVEN LETTERS OF THE MUSICAL ALPHABET

A B C D E F G

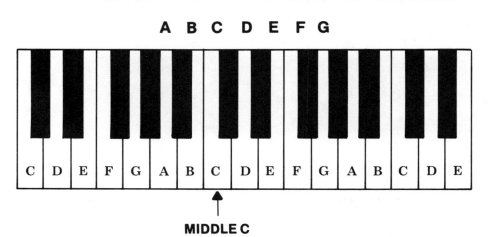

MIDDLE C

Reading from left to right, bottom to top, on the **PIANO KEYBOARD,** you will note the same lettered **WHITE KEY** is repeated every **EIGHT KEYS** - or an octave apart. **"A"** will always follow **"G", etc.**

The **WHITE KEY** directly to the left of the **TWO BLACK KEYS** is named **C. MIDDLE C** is positioned in the **CENTER** of the **PIANO KEYBOARD.**

MIDDLE C

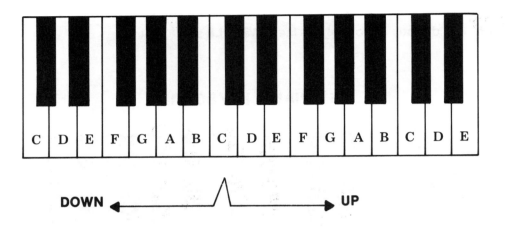

DOWN ← → **UP**

We will use **MIDDLE C** as a **DIVIDER** between the **LEFT** and **RIGHT HANDS** in our beginning studies.

FINGERING

The **THUMB** is the 1st finger of each hand . . . the numbers of the **RIGHT HAND** running from *left to right* **(UP)**, and the numbers of the **LEFT HAND** running from *right to left* **(DOWN)** in the opposite direction.

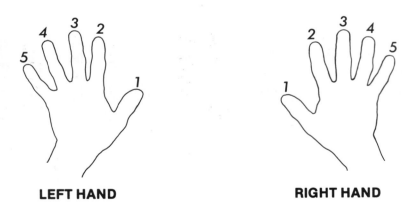

LEFT HAND　　　　　**RIGHT HAND**

Placing both **THUMBS** on **MIDDLE C**, the fingers of the **RIGHT HAND** are positioned directly over the **WHITE KEYS C—D—E—F—G** . . . and the fingers of the **LEFT HAND** are correctly positioned over the **WHITE KEYS C—B—A—G—F**, reading in the opposite direction.

Curve the fingers in a rounded fashion so that the key could be struck with the fingertips.

THE STAFF

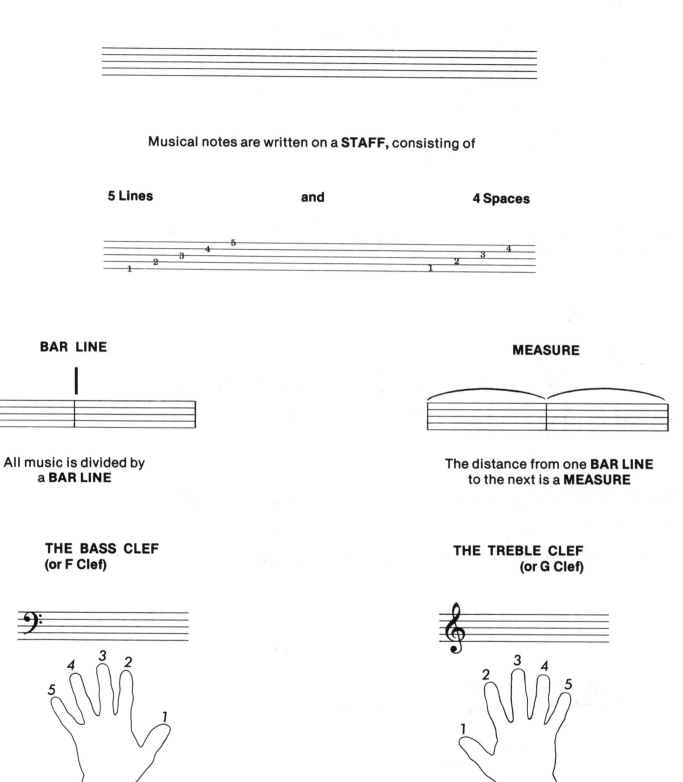

Musical notes are written on a **STAFF,** consisting of

5 Lines   and   **4 Spaces**

BAR LINE

All music is divided by
a **BAR LINE**

MEASURE

The distance from one **BAR LINE**
to the next is a **MEASURE**

THE BASS CLEF
(or F Clef)

THE TREBLE CLEF
(or G Clef)

LEFT HAND

RIGHT HAND

Early music was written on **ELEVEN LINES,** with **MIDDLE C** being the **MIDDLE LINE.** This was called

THE GRAND STAFF

— MIDDLE C LINE

Later, for convenience in reading the music for both hands, **MIDDLE C** was shown as follows, with more of a separation between each set of 5 lines. A brace connects the Treble Staff and the Bass Staff.

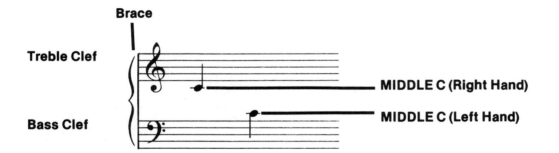

Brace

Treble Clef

MIDDLE C (Right Hand)

MIDDLE C (Left Hand)

Bass Clef

Both C's are actually the **same notes,** just spaced in relation to the **CLEF** in which they are to be played.

The **MIDDLE C** played by the **RIGHT HAND** is closest to the **TREBLE CLEF.**

THE MIDDLE C PLAYED BY THE LEFT HAND is closest to the bass clef.

THE NOTES

𝅝 = **THE WHOLE NOTE**
Hold for 4 **BEATS** OR A FULL MEASURE

𝅗𝅥 = **THE HALF NOTE**
Hold for **2 BEATS**

𝅘𝅥 = **THE QUARTER NOTE**
Hold for **1 BEAT**

MUSICAL REFRESHER # 1

1. How many groups of **TWO BLACK KEYS** do you find on the Piano Keyboard?

2. How many groups of **THREE BLACK KEYS** do you find on the Piano Keyboard?

3. Locate and play all the A's from bottom to top of the keyboard; all the B's; C's; D's; E's; F's; and G's. **NOTE** that every named **WHITE KEY** in each repeated sequence is in the same related position to a **BLACK KEY** group. This will prove a guide to help you locate any given key on the keyboard, once you are familiar with the keys.

4. Using the **MIDDLE C KEYBOARD DIAGRAM** on Page Two for correct hand positioning . . . place your **RIGHT THUMB** on **MIDDLE C** and, moving from *left to right,*

    (a) play the **WHITE KEYS C—D—E—F—G** with fingers 1 thru 5;
    (b) *reverse* the order and play **G—F—E—D—C** with fingers 5 thru 1;
    (c) play both **UP** and **DOWN** from **C** to **G** and back to **C**.
        (**REMEMBER,** the **THUMB** is the 1st finger)

5. Using the above mentioned **DIAGRAM** . . . place your **LEFT THUMB** on **MIDDLE C** and, moving from *right to left,*

    (a) play the **WHITE KEYS C—B—A—G—F** with fingers 1 thru 5;
    (b) *reverse* the order and play **F—G—A—B—C** with fingers 5 thru 1;
    (c) **NOW,** play the keys both **DOWN** and **UP** (back and forth) from **C** to **F** and back to **C**.

6. Place **BOTH THUMBS** on **MIDDLE C** and play with fingers 1 thru 5. The fingers will be moving in opposite directions . . . the right hand going **UP** and the left hand going **DOWN.** Try playing with **BOTH HANDS** moving from fingers 1 thru 5 and back to 1 again, ending on **MIDDLE C.**

7. What is the following group of 5 parallel lines called?

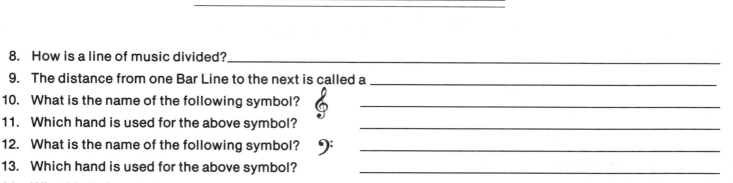

8. How is a line of music divided?_____

9. The distance from one Bar Line to the next is called a _____

10. What is the name of the following symbol?   𝄞   _____

11. Which hand is used for the above symbol?   _____

12. What is the name of the following symbol?   𝄢   _____

13. Which hand is used for the above symbol?   _____

14. What kind of a note is:

    (a) 𝅝 _____,
    (b) 𝅗𝅥 _____,
    (c) ♩ _____.

15. How many beats does each receive?

    (a) 𝅝 _____,
    (b) 𝅗𝅥 _____,
    (c) ♩ _____.

LET'S PLAY THE PIANO

NOW, we begin learning how to read music and to translate the notes we read, by way of our fingertips, to the actual keys of the piano.

You will enjoy hearing yourself first play the music you read.

TIME SIGNATURE

Each measure of music has a specified number of **BEATS** or **COUNTS.** The numbers at the beginning of a piece of study will indicate **HOW MANY BEATS** in a measure, and **WHAT KIND OF A NOTE** gets a beat.

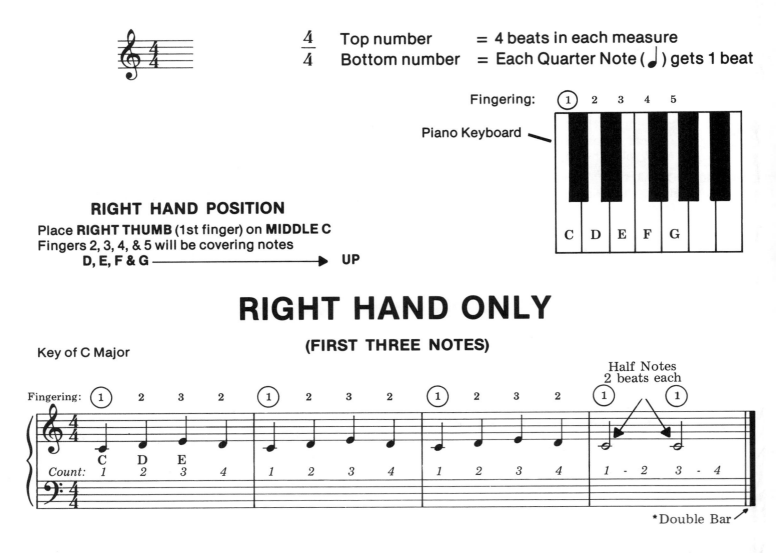

$\frac{4}{4}$ Top number = 4 beats in each measure

Bottom number = Each Quarter Note (♩) gets 1 beat

Fingering: ① 2 3 4 5

Piano Keyboard

C D E F G

RIGHT HAND POSITION

Place **RIGHT THUMB** (1st finger) on **MIDDLE C**
Fingers 2, 3, 4, & 5 will be covering notes
D, E, F & G ————————→ **UP**

RIGHT HAND ONLY

(FIRST THREE NOTES)

Key of C Major

Half Notes
2 beats each

Fingering: ① 2 3 2 ① 2 3 2 ① 2 3 2 ① ①

C D E

Count: 1 2 3 4 1 2 3 4 1 2 3 4 1 - 2 3 - 4

*Double Bar

Keep the hand in position over the proper keys at all times, lifting each finger and striking the note firmly.

Count evenly as you play and hold each note down for its full value.

***THE DOUBLE BAR** is always used at the **END** of a piece or study.

8

Fingering:

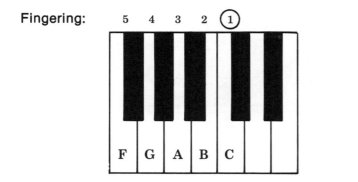

LEFT HAND POSITION
Place **LEFT HAND** (1st finger) on **MIDDLE C**
Fingers 2, 3, 4 & 5 will be covering notes
B, A, G & F
DOWN ◄——————————— (played right to left)

LEFT HAND ONLY

(FIRST THREE NOTES)

Follow direction of notes

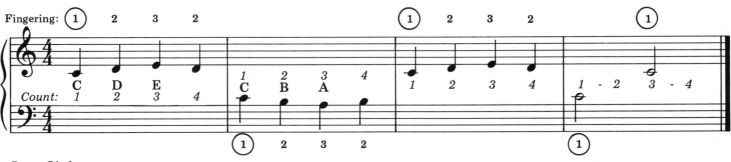

Fingering:

BOTH HANDS   **AT MIDDLE C**

TWO HANDS

(THREE NOTES)

Treble Clef

Bass Clef

MORE BOTH HANDS

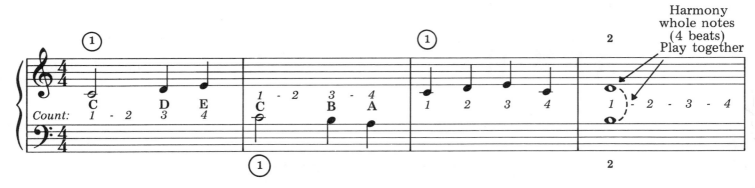

The **TWO WHOLE NOTES** as played with both hands give you the first sound of **HARMONY** . . . .

FIVE FINGERS, FIVE NOTES

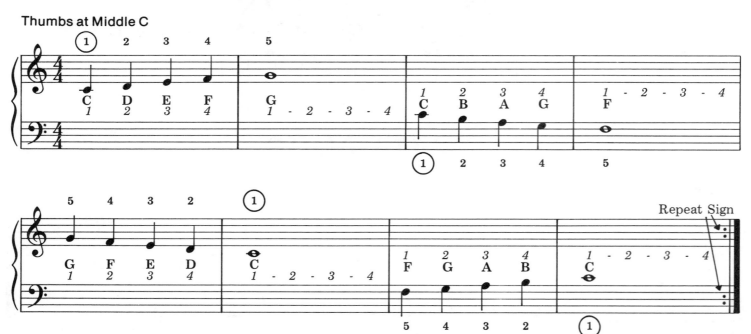

REPEAT SIGN: Double Bar with the Two Dots, meaning **GO BACK TO THE BEGINNING AND PLAY AGAIN** . . .
do not lose the count (beats) when you do so.

A NEW TIME SIGNATURE

$\frac{2}{4}$ Top number   = 2 beats in each measure
      Bottom number   = Each Quarter Note (♩) gets 1 beat

SKIPPING AROUND

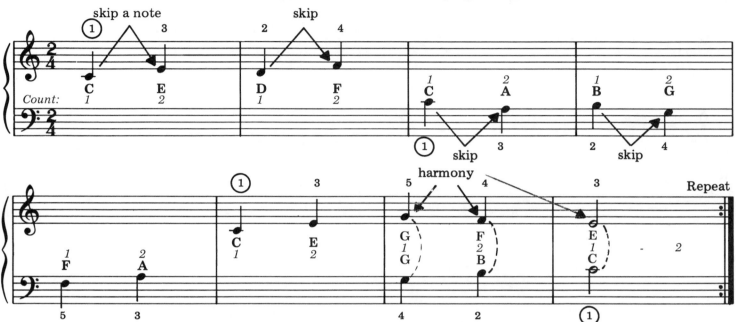

As you play the above exercise, note the **CONTRARY MOTION** in the last two measures. The Right Hand is moving **DOWN** and the Left Hand **UP**. Hands move in opposite directions.

It is good practice to **COUNT ALOUD** as you play each study.

TO AND FRO

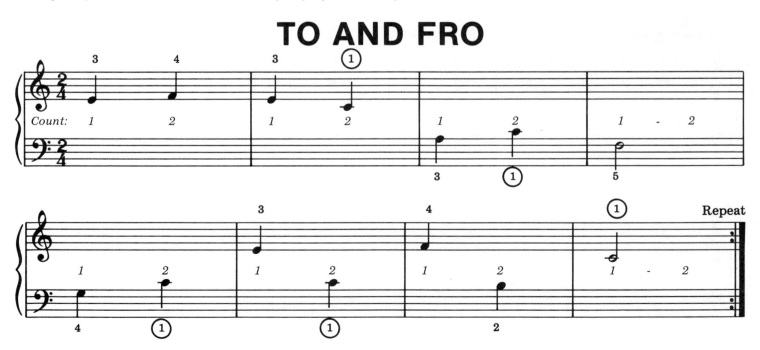

RIGHT AND LEFT

RUNNING BACKWARDS

CONTRARY MOTION

C = Common Time

(Same as $\frac{4}{4}$)

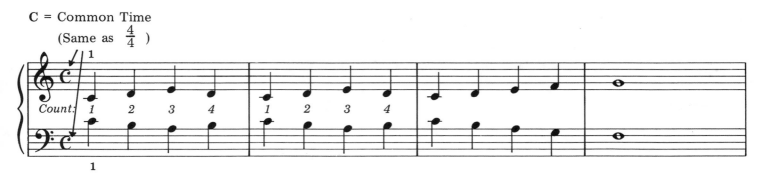

SAME DIRECTION

PRACTICE SUGGESTIONS:

Play above exercises at least 5 times for smooth playing.

ALSO, it is always a good idea to repeat the studies on previous pages several times each, for perfection.

RESTS

A **REST** is a sign of **SILENCE** in music

We count the beats but do not play

Lift the fingers when you come to a **REST**

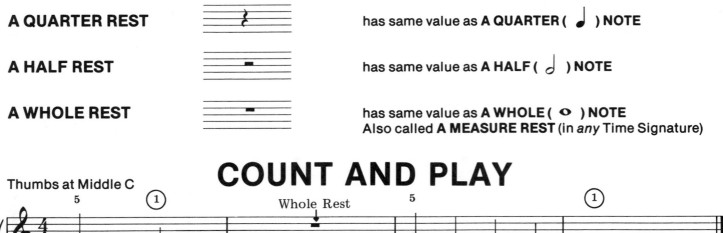

A QUARTER REST   has same value as **A QUARTER (♩) NOTE**

A HALF REST   has same value as **A HALF (♩) NOTE**

A WHOLE REST   has same value as **A WHOLE (𝅝) NOTE**
Also called **A MEASURE REST** (in *any* Time Signature)

COUNT AND PLAY

HERE'S THE REST

PRACTICE SUGGESTION:

(1) Play through and count the beats
(2) On the **REPEAT,** name the notes in both hands

14

Further study of the **RESTS**

PARADE REST
(Quarter and Measure Rests)

STROLLING THRU THE PARK
(Half and Whole Rests)

PRACTICE SUGGESTION:

Play over the above exercises and those on previous pages at least **FIVE TIMES** for satisfactory results.

THE DOT (.)

A DOT PLACED AFTER A NOTE ADDS ONE-HALF OF THE VALUE TO THE NOTE

Example: THE DOTTED HALF NOTE ♩. = 3 BEATS

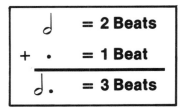

$$\begin{array}{rl} \text{♩} & = \text{2 Beats} \\ + \quad . & = \text{1 Beat} \\ \hline \text{♩.} & = \text{3 Beats} \end{array}$$

A NEW TIME SIGNATURE

$\dfrac{3}{4}$ = 3 beats in each measure

$\dfrac{3}{4}$ = Each Quarter Note (♩) gets 1 beat

THIS IS CALLED WALTZ TIME

THE TIE

A CURVED LINE CONNECTING TWO NOTES OF THE SAME PITCH.
Play the first note and hold for the value of both notes.

THE WALTZ

REMEMBER...

The **WHOLE REST** signifies a **WHOLE MEASURE OF SILENCE** in **ANY TIME SIGNATURE.**

YOUR FIRST MELODY
MELODY: A TUNE or THEME

Introducing the PHRASE or SLUR:

A curved line over or under a group of notes indicating the notes are to be played smoothly, as a Musical Sentence.

A SIMPLE MELODY

Key of C Major
Hand Position: Thumbs at Middle C

MATT DENNIS a.s.c.a.p.

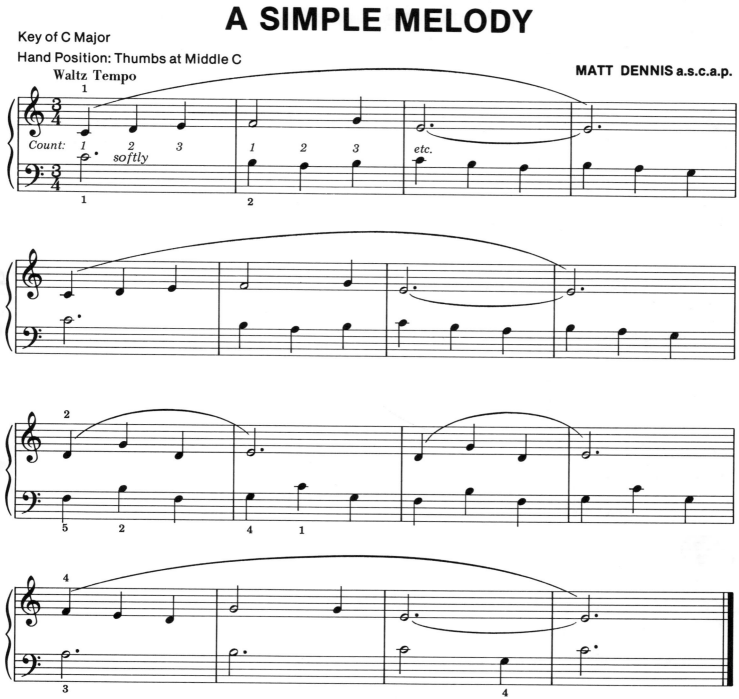

A MELODY DIVIDED BETWEEN HANDS... follow the dotted lines

SOFTLY, THE WIND
(FOLK SONG STYLE)

Lyric and Music by
MATT DENNIS a.s.c.a.p.

1st ENDING means to **REPEAT** piece from beginning, then **SKIP** to *2nd ENDING.*

MUSICAL TERMS: **MODERATO =** Play at a **MODERATE** or **MEDIUM SPEED**

p (piano)   = **SOFT**

legato   = **SMOOTHLY**

FOLK SONGS: Simple songs describing scenes or activities of daily life of the people, such as work, play, love, patriotic, dancing, cradle, mourning, narrative and epic songs, etc.

MUSICAL REFRESHER # 2

1. What is a **TIME SIGNATURE?**
2. How many beats in a measure of $\frac{2}{4}$ time? $\frac{3}{4}$ time? $\frac{4}{4}$ time?
3. What is a **DOUBLE BAR?**
4. Notes played together are called an _____.
5. The **DOUBLE BAR** with **TWO DOTS** is called a _____(two words)
6. What is the meaning of a **REPEAT SIGN?**
7. Explain **CONTRARY MOTION** between hands, at the piano.
8. What is a **REST?** _____
9. What kind of **RESTS** are the following, and how many beats does each receive?

_____   _____   _____

10. The **TIME SIGNATURE** of C is called_____(two words)
    This is the same as what kind of **TIME?** _____
11. What is the meaning of the **DOT?**_____
12. What kind of a note is the following?

    How many beats does this note have? _____
13. $\frac{3}{4}$ **TIME** is also called_____(two words)
14. What is the following symbol? _____

15. What is a **MELODY?**_____
16. Define a **PHRASE** or **SLUR.** _____
17. What is a **FOLK SONG?** _____
18. Describe 1st and 2nd **ENDINGS.** _____
19. In the **TIME SIGNATURE** of 3/4 what kind of **REST** denotes a **WHOLE MEASURE** of silence? _____
20. Give the meaning of the following **MUSICAL TERMS:**
    (1) **MODERATO** _____
    (2) *p* (piano) _____
    (3) *legato* _____

Fingering: 5 4 3 2 ①

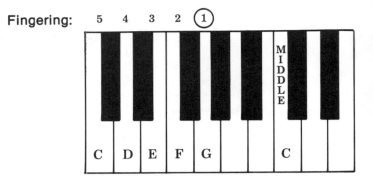

A NEW POSITION FOR LEFT HAND
C—G (Below MIDDLE C)
Thumb on G

ON THE MOVE

Play with Left Hand Only

BOTH HANDS ON THE MOVE

PRACTICE SUGGESTION:

Play the above several times each until the fingers move evenly and with flexibility.

REMEMBER to hold the hands in a natural, rounded position **ABOVE** the keyboard, and play the keys with the **TIPS** of the fingers.

SPREADING OUT

Right Hand C — G
Left Hand C — G (C below Middle C)

PLAY OVER the above exercise several times, until fingers work smoothly and you become familiar with the new expanded Left Hand Position.

8 NOTES APART
(THE OCTAVE INTERVAL)

OCTAVE: Same lettered notes, 8 notes apart, played together.
This is an **INTERVAL.**

READING THE NOTES ON THE
LINES AND SPACES
(5)   (4)

Treble Clef:

LINES   SPACES

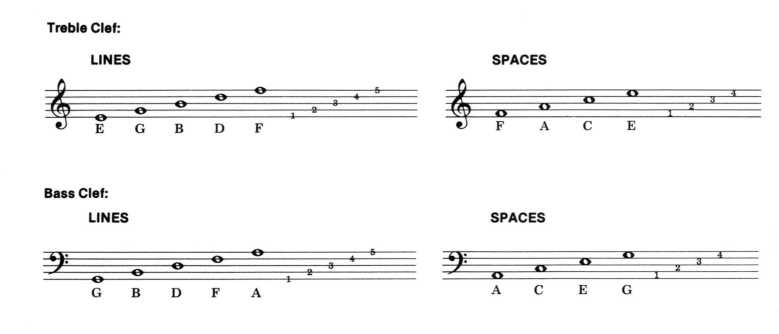

E   G   B   D   F   F   A   C   E

Bass Clef:

LINES   SPACES

G   B   D   F   A   A   C   E   G

IMPORTANT NOTES

In the **TREBLE CLEF,** the note of *D* is directly *below* the bottom or 1st line of the staff . . . or, reading *up,* in between **MIDDLE C** and the 1st line of **E.**

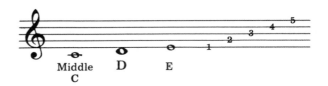

Middle C   D   E

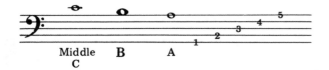

Middle C   B   A

In the **BASS CLEF,** the note of *B* is directly *above* the top or 5th line of the staff . . . or, reading *down,* in between **MIDDLE C** and the 5th line of *A.*

MEMORIZE THE ABOVE, AND YOU WILL BE ABLE TO SIGHT-READ AND PLAY THE NOTES WITH EASE IN FUTURE STUDIES AND PIECES.

EXERCISE SUGGESTION:

Find the notes on the *Keyboard* for the **LINES AND SPACES** of the **TREBLE** and **BASS CLEFS,** plus the other **IMPORTANT NOTES,** as shown above.

NAME, LOCATE AND PLAY THE FOLLOWING
Disregard "Hand Position" and Fingering for these Exercises

LINE NOTES

Treble Clef (R.H.)

Bass Clef (L.H.)

SPACE NOTES

Treble Clef (R.H.)

Bass Clef (L.H.)

LINES AND SPACES

R.H.

L.H.

EIGHTH NOTES

THE EIGHTH NOTE ♪ has half the value of a Quarter Note
Two Eighth Notes make a Quarter Note

Two or more are written

♪ = ½ BEAT
♪♪ = 1 BEAT (♩)

Count by dividing the Quarter into two parts such as

" 1 and 2 and etc."

THREE PIECES OF EIGHT

Key of C Major
Hand Positions: C—G

MATT DENNIS a.s.c.a.p.

1
COPPER

In 2/4 Moderate Tempo

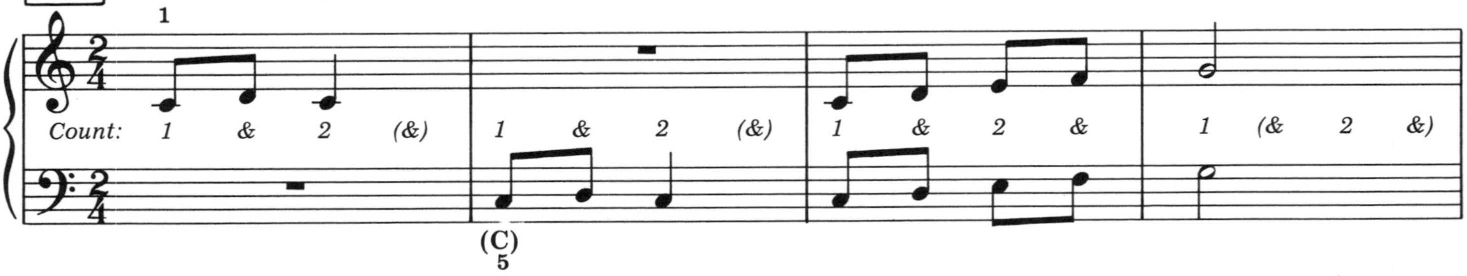

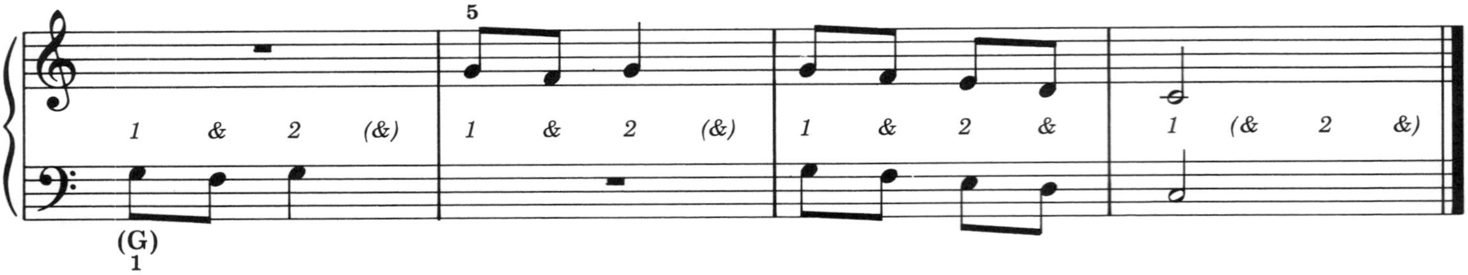

Count: 1 & 2 (&) | 1 & 2 (&) | 1 & 2 & | 1 (& 2 &)

(C)
5

1 & 2 (&) | 1 & 2 (&) | 1 & 2 & | 1 (& 2 &)

(G)
1

TEMPO: The speed of a composition, fast or slow.

2
SILVER

In 4/4 Moderato

Fine

1 & 2 (&) 3 & 4 (&) | 1 & 2 & 3 (& 4 &) | etc.

5

INTERVAL: 2 notes together, also called a Double Note.

*D.C. al Fine (Da Capo al Fine):
    Go back to the beginning and play to the word "Fine" (End).

3
GOLD

Fermata

© Copyright 1977 by Matt Dennis a.s.c.a.p.
International Copyright Secured. Made In U.S.A. All Rights Reserved

rit. (ritardando) = GRADUALLY SLOWER
FERMATA ⌒ = HOLD OR PAUSE

THE INTERVAL
(2 NOTE HARMONY)

The **INTERVAL** is determined by counting **UPWARD** the number of steps from the lower named note to the higher named note. **INTERVALS** can **START** on **ANY** note.

Play over the following examples several times with the **RIGHT HAND** before playing the complete study below with **BOTH HANDS**.

INTERVAL NUMBER NAMES

PLAY OVER several times in a steady rhythm, then **NAME THE INTERVALS** as you play them at an even tempo. Note difference between **MELODIC** and **HARMONIC**.

To Strengthen The Fingers

(Play With A Steady Rhythm)

WARMING UP

Shift hands *up* to next **WHITE KEY** with each new exercise.

Play smoothly with a steady beat.

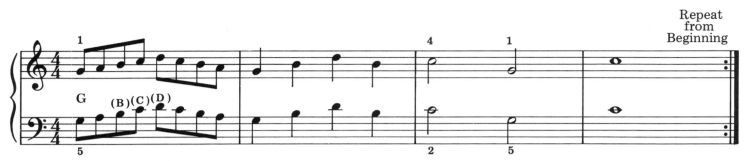

PRACTICE SUGGESTION:

Play the above exercise completely through, go back to the beginning and play again. To really limber up the fingers, play **EACH LINE** separately, at least 5 times before advancing to the next line.

TAKING OFF

CLIMBING UP

REPEAT above exercises several times for smooth playing.
REMEMBER TO CURVE FINGERS and play with tips of fingers for proper position.

JET POWER

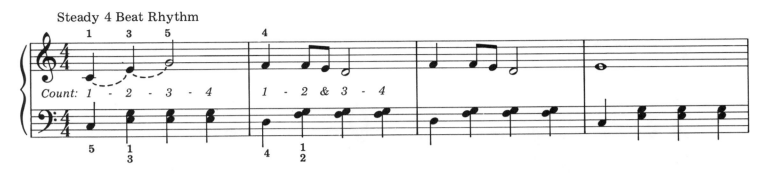

SMOOTH FLYING

Quarter
Rest

Play on 2nd & 4th Beats,
called "AFTERBEATS"

PRACTICE SUGGESTION:

REPEAT THE ABOVE SERIES AT LEAST 5 TIMES EACH.

A COLORFUL, NEW DIMENSION OF SOUND IS OURS AS WE NOW LEARN TO READ AND PLAY...

THE SHARP ♯

To play a **SHARP** ♯... **RAISE** the note a half step (to a black or white note)

F to F♯   B to B♯
(Same as C)

THE FLAT ♭

To play a **FLAT** ♭ ... **LOWER** the note a half step (to a black or white note)

D to D♭   F to F♭
(Same as E)

OBSERVE THAT THE *SHARP* ♯ **YOU PLAY GOING** *UP* **THE KEYBOARD**
BECOMES THE *FLAT* ♭ **AS YOU RETURN** *DOWN* **THE KEYBOARD ...**
THE NOTES CAN HAVE *TWO DIFFERENT NAMES.*

THE NATURAL

A **NATURAL** ♮ will **CANCEL** a sharp or flat.   To play a **NATURAL** ♮ ... play a white key.

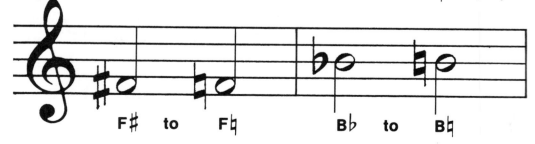

F♯   to   F♮   B♭   to   B♮

SHARPS, FLATS AND NATURALS

NAME THE FOLLOWING NOTES AND LOCATE ON THE PIANO KEYBOARD.

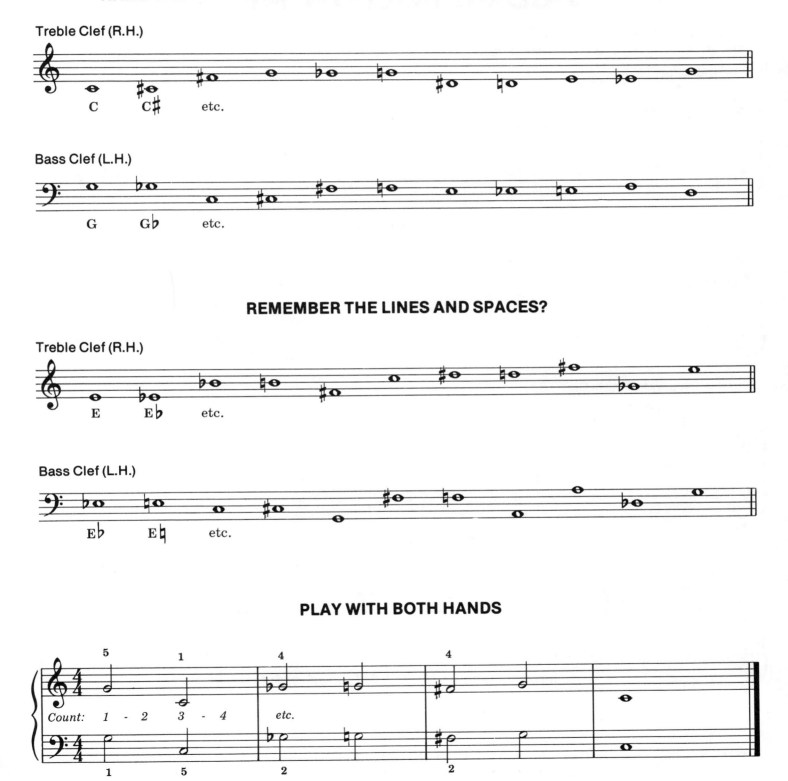

REMEMBER THE LINES AND SPACES?

PLAY WITH BOTH HANDS

THE SHARP ♯, FLAT ♭ , OR NATURAL ♮ AFFECTS ANY REPEATED NOTES ON THE SAME LINE OR SPACE IN THE SAME MEASURE.

COME FOLLOW ME

RIGHT HAND: C—G Then **C—G** one octave (8 notes) higher.
LEFT HAND: C—G Then **C—G** one octave (8 notes) higher (in Treble Clef).

MATT DENNIS a.s.c.a.p.

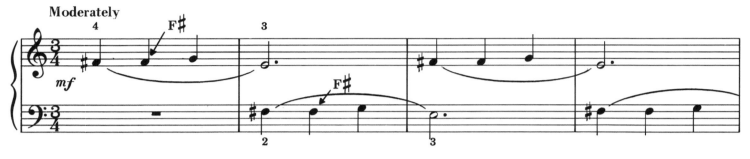

Both Hands play in Treble Clef

NOTE STEMS (Rule) = STEMS *UP* ON RIGHT SIDE OF NOTES *BELOW MIDDLE LINE.*
STEMS *DOWN* ON LEFT SIDE OF NOTES *ON OR ABOVE MIDDLE LINE.*

mf (mezzo forte) = **MEDIUM LOUD**

KEY OF G MAJOR

F SHARP (F#) KEY SIGNATURE
(Every F is sharped)

CIRCUS PARADE

R.H. D—A
L.H. G—D (5th finger extension to F#)

MATT DENNIS a.s.c.a.p.

Tempo di Marcia

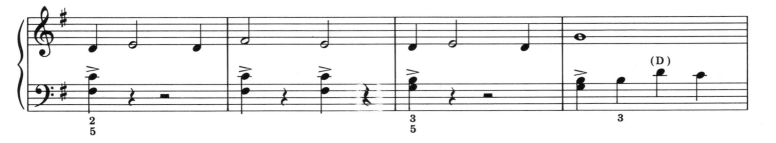

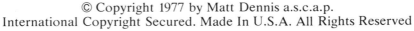

TEMPO DI MARCIA = **A MARCH,** play with a strong beat and with spirit
f (Forte) = **LOUD**
> (ACCENT) = Strike notes more firmly, **LOUDER.**

BREAKING AWAY FROM THE FIXED HAND POSITIONS FOR AN EXPANDED PLAYING RANGE OF NOTES. . . WATCH FINGERING CHANGES, SHARPS, FLATS AND NATURALS.

WINGS OF LOVE

Key of **G** Major
Remember the F# Key Signature
R.H. Starting position G—D
L.H. Starting position G—D

MATT DENNIS a.s.c.a.p.

mp (mezzo piano) = **MEDIUM SOFT**
DYNAMICS (Volume) :
cresc. (Crescendo) = **GRADUALLY LOUDER**
dim. (Diminuendo) = **GRADUALLY SOFTER**

STRETCHING, OR REACHING OUT FOR A NOTE FROM ANY HAND POSITION

INTRODUCING: (1) "Staccato" — The short accented note ( ).

                  (2) "Thumb Under" — For flexible finger movement.

                  (3) "Finger Change" — On same note.

FUNNY LITTLE TUNE

Key of C Major

Starting Hand Positions:
R.H. Thumb on E, watch fingering changes.
L.H. C—G (Thumb under), watch fingering changes.

MATT DENNIS a.s.c.a.p.

WHEN YOU SMILE AT ME

MATT DENNIS a.s.c.a.p.

Hand Position:
R.H. F—C
L.H. F—C

ANDANTE MODERATO	= **MODERATELY SLOW**
INCOMPLETE MEASURE	= The *beginning* measure has an insufficient number of beats . . . the *last* measure of the study will provide the missing beats. In the above 4/4 time the "Pick Up Notes" are to be played on the 4th beat.
"PICK UP NOTES"	= The opening notes of a melodic phrase, starting in an Incomplete Measure preceding the first regular measure. Count the Silent Beats to yourself and start to play on beats indicated, to establish the rhythm of the piece or study.

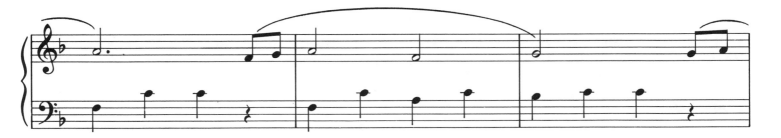

Incomplete Measure
See Beginning "Pick-Up Notes"

NOTE . . . In the following study in 2/4 time the "Pick Up Notes" are to be played on the 2nd beat of the beginning Incomplete Measure. Count the 1st beat silently, to yourself, to correctly set the tempo.

A FRENCH DANCE
(17th CENTURY STYLE BOURREE)

Key of F Major
Bb Key Signature
No set hand position
Observe fingering

MATT DENNIS a.s.c.a.p.

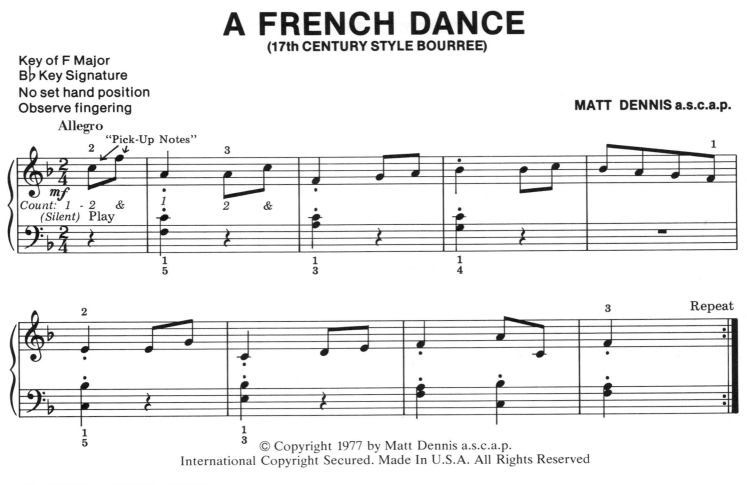

ALLEGRO = LIVELY, JOYFUL

ACCIDENTALS

YOU HAVE BEEN PLAYING SOME ACCIDENTALS IN PREVIOUS PIECES. . .SHARPS #'s, FLATS b's AND NATURALS ♮'s USED FOR SINGLE NOTES <u>OTHER THAN KEY SIGNATURE NOTES</u>, AND EFFECTIVE ONLY FOR THE MEASURE IN WHICH THEY ARE WRITTEN.

EXAMPLES:

1. The **KEY OF F MAJOR** has a **B** b **KEY SIGNATURE**, meaning in this Key every **B** is *flatted* unless cancelled by a *Natural* (Accidental).

ACCIDENTALS ARE CIRCLED

2. Likewise, in the **KEY OF G MAJOR** there is an **F# KEY SIGNATURE**, which means every **F** is *sharped* unless cancelled by a *Natural* (Accidental).

ACCIDENTALS ARE CIRCLED

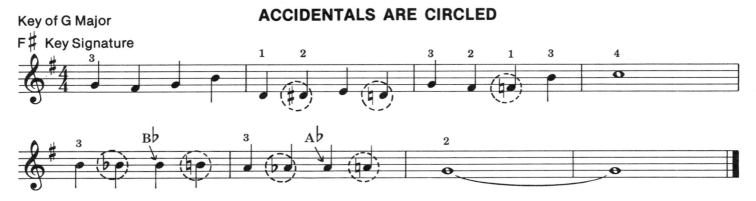

3. The **KEY OF C MAJOR** has **NO** sharps or flats in the Key Signature. **ALL** sharps, flats and naturals would be **ACCIDENTALS**.

ACCIDENTALS ARE CIRCLED

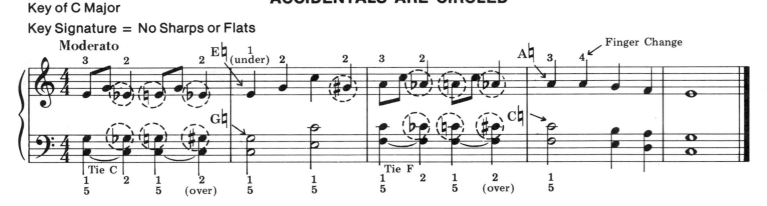

THE DOTTED QUARTER NOTE

REMEMBER THE RULE FOR THE *DOT?* **PLACED AFTER A NOTE THE DOT ADDS ONE HALF OF THE VALUE TO THE NOTE.**

IN 2/4, 3/4, AND 4/4 TIME THE DOTTED QUARTER NOTE = 1½ BEATS

$\quad\bd = $ 1 Beat

$+\quad\cdot = $ ½ Beat

$\quad\bd\cdot = $ 1½ Beats

HOLD THE NOTE FOR 1½ BEATS . . . The **DOT** represents the first half of the count of **TWO** ②

SONG OF FAITH

Key of F Major
B♭ Key Signature
Observe fingering

MATT DENNIS a.s.c.a.p.

Andante—Spiritual

ANDANTE = PLAY SLOWLY   **SPIRITUAL = A SONG OF FAITH**

REMINDER: The **SLUR** is a curved line connecting two or more **DIFFERENT** notes, to be played legato.

AN EIGHTH REST   ≡ 𝄾 ≡   = ½ Beat   same value as AN EIGHTH (♪) NOTE

The following is an example of a **POPULAR** styled piece in 32 measure form. Popular Music, however, can vary in measure length depending upon Melodic structure. Note use of the **EIGHTH REST, DOTTED QUARTER NOTE, PHRASE MARKINGS, HARMONIC INTERVALS, SHIFTING HAND POSITIONS, SPECIAL FINGERING,** and be sure to **REMEMBER** that F# is the **KEY SIGNATURE** of the **KEY OF G MAJOR.**

FEELIN' GOOD

Composed and Arranged by
MATT DENNIS a.s.c.a.p.

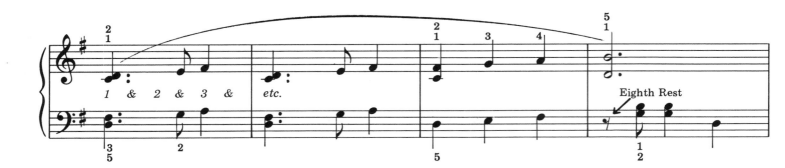

MUSICAL REFRESHER #3

1. What is an **OCTAVE**? _____
2. Name the **LINES** and **SPACES**: a. The **TREBLE CLEF** _____
                                b. The **BASS CLEF** _____
3. The note on the 4th **LINE** of the **TREBLE CLEF** is _____.
4. The note on the 5th **LINE** of the **BASS CLEF** is _____.
5. The note on the 4th **SPACE** of the **TREBLE CLEF** is _____.
6. What kind of a note is ____♪____ and what **BEAT** does it receive? _____
7. Define **TEMPO.** _____
8. **D.C. al FINE** means _____
9. What is the meaning of the following?
   rit._____ **FERMATA** ⌢ _____
10. An **INTERVAL** is made up of_____notes.
11. Name the following **INTERVALS** by **NUMBERS**:

12. For correct playing form should you play the notes on the keyboard with the flat part or tips of the fingers?
    _____
13. How do you play a **SHARP**? _____
    A FLAT?_____**A NATURAL?**_____
14. Does a **SHARP, FLAT** or **NATURAL** hold good for **REPEATED NOTES** on same line or space in same measure?
    (Yes or No)_____
15. What does *mf* mean? _____
16. Give the **RULE** for **STEMS** on notes. _____
17. Name the **KEY** with **ONE SHARP** in the **KEY SIGNATURE**, and **NAME THE SHARP.** _____
18. What is **TEMPO di MARCIA?** _____
19. Define the meaning of the following signs and terms:
    *f*_____   >_____   *mp*_____
    cresc. ◁_____   dim. ▷_____
20. What is the meaning of **ANDANTE MODERATO?** _____
21. **"PICK UP NOTES"** are _____.
22. An **INCOMPLETE MEASURE** is _____.
23. **ALLEGRO** means **LIVELY** or **SLOWLY?** _____
24. **STACCATO** indicates a note should be played _____
25. What are **ACCIDENTALS?** _____
26. What is the **KEY SIGNATURE** of the **KEY OF C MAJOR?** _____
27. The **DOTTED QUARTER NOTE** ♩. gets_____beats.
28. Name the **KEY** with **ONE FLAT** in the **KEY SIGNATURE**, and **NAME THE FLAT.** _____
29. What kind of **REST** is the following, ▬ and what **BEAT** does it receive? _____

BOTH HANDS PLAYING IN THE TREBLE CLEF

Remember THE LINES and THE SPACES

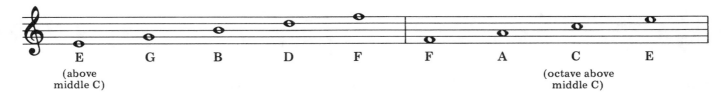

E   G   B   D   F   F   A   C   E

(above middle C)   (octave above middle C)

LITTLE DUTCH GIRL

MATT DENNIS a.s.c.a.p.

R.H. starting position C — G (octave above Middle C)
L.H. starting position C — G (Middle C)

REPEAT THIS PIECE A FEW TIMES . . . GOOD PRACTICE FOR PLAYING **"THIRDS"**.

BOTH HANDS PLAYING IN THE BASS CLEF

Remember **THE LINES** and **THE SPACES**

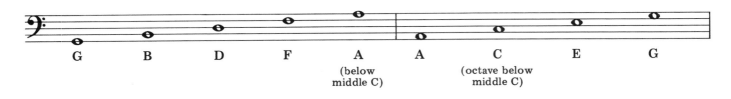

G B D F A A C E G

(below middle C) (octave below middle C)

NICE TO KNOW YA!

R.H. position E — B (below Middle C)
L.H. starting position G — D (Bottom Line G)

**Lyric and Music by
MATT DENNIS a.s.c.a.p.**

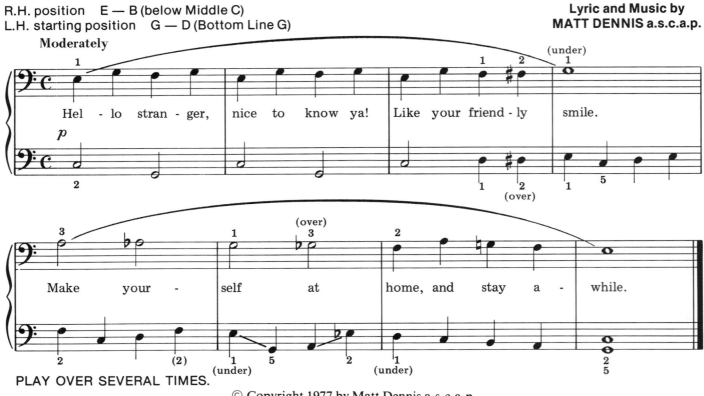

Hel - lo stran - ger, nice to know ya! Like your friend - ly smile.

Make your - self at home, and stay a - while.

PLAY OVER SEVERAL TIMES.

To correctly play and understand the many interesting sounding **CHORDS** used in **POPULAR MUSIC**, as well as to learn how to play in different **KEYS**, we must first **MEMORIZE**

THE MAJOR SCALE PATTERN

A series of 8 notes, steps or degrees, in alphabetical order, beginning and ending on the same named note, in a pattern of **WHOLE** and **HALF STEPS.** The **HALF STEPS** are between 3 and 4, and 7 and 8; all the rest are **WHOLE STEPS.** Note that we will use Roman Numerals for convenience in constructing **CHORDS.**

A Scale can start on ANY note, the pattern remains the same.

ALL CHORDS are based on, or relative to, **THE MAJOR SCALE PATTERN.**

W = Whole Step   H = Half Step

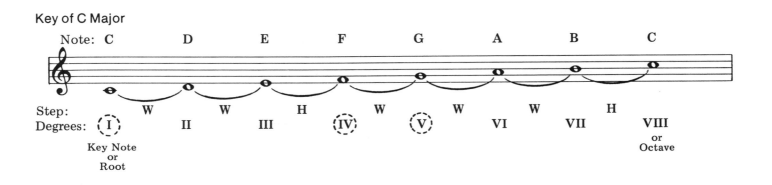

Key of C Major

PLAYING THE MAJOR SCALE

SCALES have special fingering, depending upon the starting note. As you play the one octave (8 note) scale below, in the Key of C Major, you will notice the **1st finger (thumb)** reaches **UNDER** as you play **UP** the scale in the **TREBLE CLEF** ... and the **3rd finger** crosses **OVER** on your return **DOWN.**

In the **BASS CLEF**, your **3rd finger** crosses **OVER** on the way **UP**, and your **1st (thumb)** reaches **UNDER** on the way **DOWN** the scale.

Practice the following exercises several times, while you count the **TIME** evenly, until you can play, with both hands, in a well coordinated manner.

RIGHT HAND ONLY (Treble Clef)

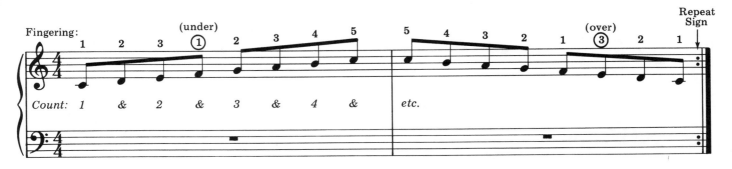

2. LEFT HAND ONLY (Bass Clef)

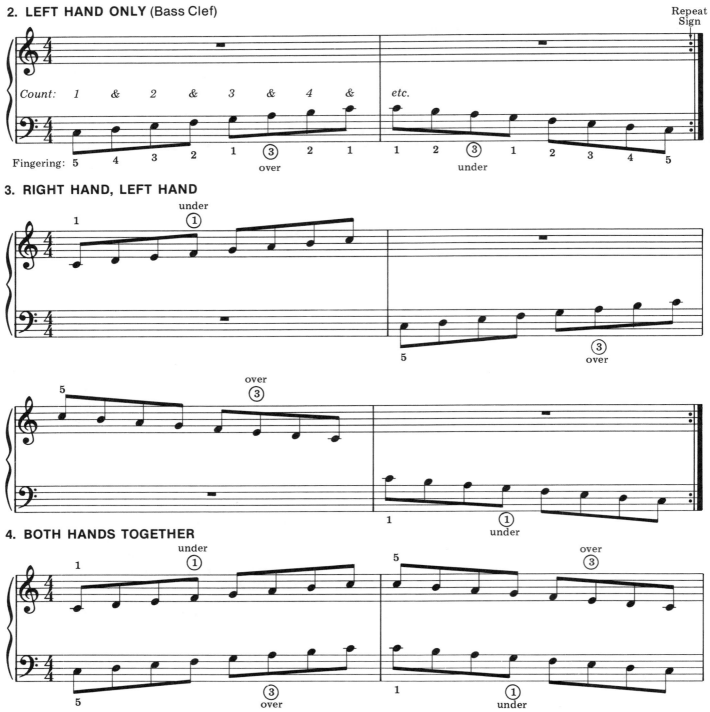

3. RIGHT HAND, LEFT HAND

4. BOTH HANDS TOGETHER

FINGER FLEXIBILITY

1 and 3, UNDER AND OVER

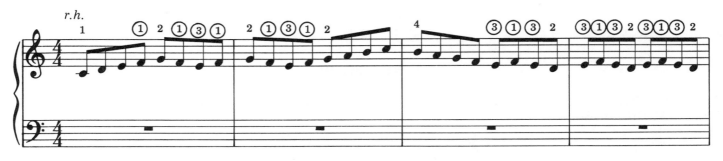

3 and 1, OVER AND UNDER

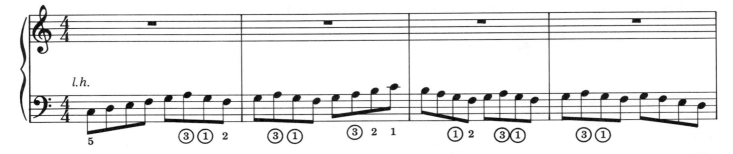

PRACTICE THE ABOVE EXERCISES AT LEAST 5 TIMES DAILY.

THE TRIAD

A **TRIAD** is a **CHORD** of three notes . . . the 1st, 3rd and 5th notes of a scale. For example, in the Key of C Major the **TRIAD** would be formed of   C   E   G.

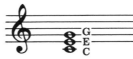

INVERSIONS

There are **THREE** positions of a **TRIAD**, meaning we may change the order of the notes. This is called **INVERTING THE TRIAD OR CHORD.**

You will notice we moved the bottom note (C) to the top of the next **TRIAD** or **CHORD** position, making this the **1st Inversion.** Likewise, we moved the bottom note (E) of *this* **TRIAD** TO THE TOP OF THE *NEXT* **TRIAD** position, making this one the **2nd Inversion.** The notes move an octave each time.

"BROKEN CHORD"

Some studies or pieces will show the **TRIAD** to be played with one note following the other. We call this a **"BROKEN CHORD".**

C   E   G   or   E   G   C   etc.

"BLOCKED CHORD"

When the notes are played together, this is called a **"BLOCKED CHORD".**

etc.

Key of C Major — The C Major Triad

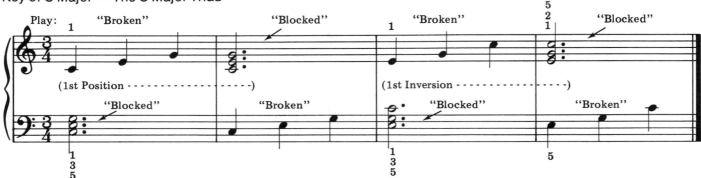

PRACTICE SUGGESTION: Figure out and play the **TRIADS** of Keys of C, F and G Major and play the Positions and Inversions of each **TRIAD.**

REMEMBER THE MAJOR SCALE PATTERN . . . in figuring out the **MAJOR TRIADS,** and you will recall **A SCALE CAN START ON ANY NOTE — THE PATTERN REMAINS THE SAME.**

6/8 TIME

A NEW TIME SIGNATURE

We learned that in 2/4, 3/4 and 4/4 Time Signatures, the Quarter note (♩) receives **ONE** beat or count.

In 6/8 Time, the **EIGHTH** note (♪) receives **ONE** beat.

$\dfrac{6}{8}$ 6 = 6 beats to a measure
8 = Eighth note (♪) gets 1 beat

♪ = 1 beat

♩ = 2 beats   ♩ = 4 beats

♩. = 3 beats   ♩. = 6 beats

Accordingly, the **RESTS** have *this* value (in 6/8 Time):

Eighth Rest   (𝄾)   = 1 beat
Quarter Rest (𝄽)   = 2 beats
Whole Rest   (▬)   = Whole measure

Play and count the time of this lively 6/8 rhythm:

Key of F Major (B♭ Signature)

By MATT DENNIS a.s.c.a.p.

Allegro — With Spirit

SOUND THE CALL TO SEA
(A BUGLE CALL)

After repeat, continue to next strain

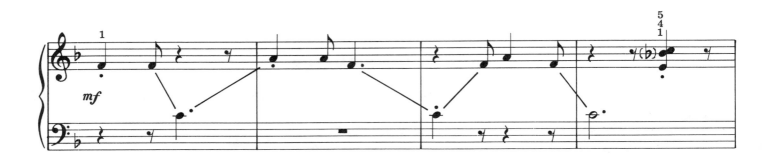

D.C. al fine

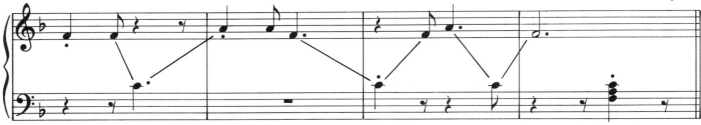

REMINDER: D.C. al fine = Go back to beginning and play to word "fine".

CASCADES

Key of C Major

By MATT DENNIS a.s.c.a.p.

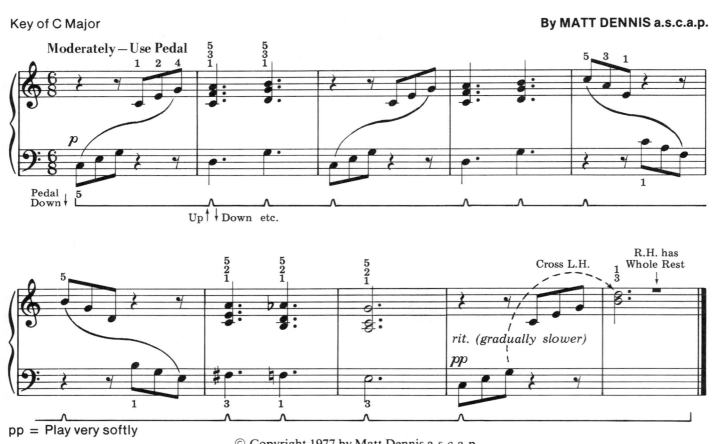

Pedal Down ↓ 5

Up↑ ↓Down etc.

Cross L.H.

R.H. has Whole Rest

rit. (gradually slower)

pp = Play very softly

OUTER LEDGER LINE NOTES ABOVE THE TREBLE STAFF

PLAYED BY THE RIGHT HAND

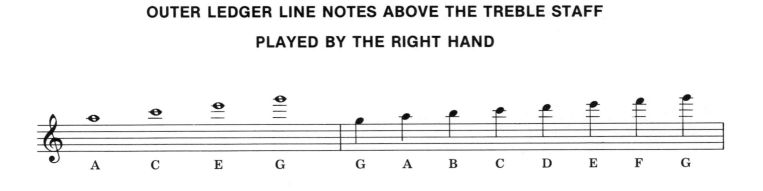

THEME FOR "RIGHTY"

R.H. plays melody
L.H. plays accompaniment in **TREBLE CLEF**

By MATT DENNIS a.s.c.a.p.

OUTER LEDGER LINE NOTES BELOW THE BASS CLEF STAFF
PLAYED BY THE LEFT HAND

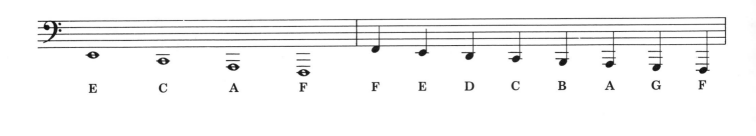

E C A F   F E D C B A G F

DENIZENS OF THE DEEP

L.H. plays melody
R.H. plays accompaniment in **BASS CLEF**

By MATT DENNIS a.s.c.a.p.

Key of F Major (The B is flatted in this piece - except for the "accidental")

(D minor)

Slowly

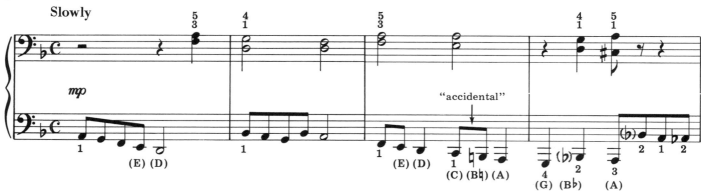

D MINOR = Relative Minor to Key of F Major
        See explanation under **MINOR KEYS AND CHORDS,** further in this book.

INNER LEDGER LINE NOTES ABOVE THE BASS CLEF STAFF
PLAYED BY THE LEFT HAND

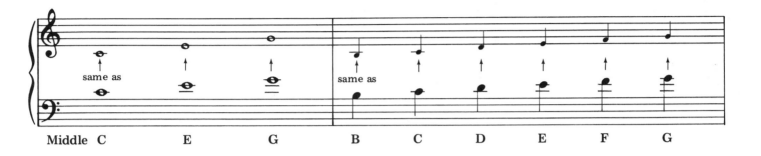

Middle C   E   G   B   C   D   E   F   G

THEME FOR "LEFTY"

L.H. plays melody
R.H. plays accompaniment

By MATT DENNIS a.s.c.a.p.

INNER LEDGER LINE NOTES BELOW THE TREBLE CLEF STAFF
PLAYED BY THE RIGHT HAND

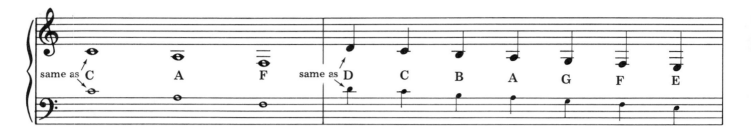

RIDIN' IN ON A WAVE

By MATT DENNIS a.s.c.a.p.

IN **POPULAR MUSIC** it may at times be necessary to play single notes or chords with the Right Hand, written **BELOW THE TREBLE CLEF.** Practice the above several times and become familiar with the placement of these notes in relation to the Bass Clef.

THE TRIPLET...

THREE notes played in the time of **TWO** notes *of the same value,* connected by a *slur,* with a small numeral *3.*

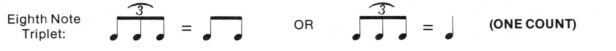

Eighth Note Triplet:

THE TRIPLET is commonly used in all forms of music, including **POPULAR**. In the following piece the **TRIPLET** of three eighth notes receives the same time value as two eighth notes, or **ONE COUNT** (a quarter note beat).

WISH ME LOVE

Andante espressivo (slowly, with expression)

By MATT DENNIS a.s.c.a.p.

DAMPER PEDAL: the pedal to your **RIGHT,** used to sustain the tones. Correctly used, press pedal down down immediately **after** the note is struck. Practice will make this a natural habit.

The words "pedal simile" mean to continue with the *same pattern* of using the pedal.

NOTE: PLEASE OBSERVE where **MELODY** shifts to L.H. in the 9th measure, then back to R.H. in 15th measure.

REMEMBER: If a note is changed by an accidental within the measure, the accidental holds good for the rest of the measure.

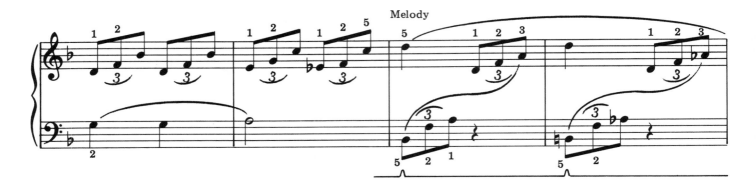

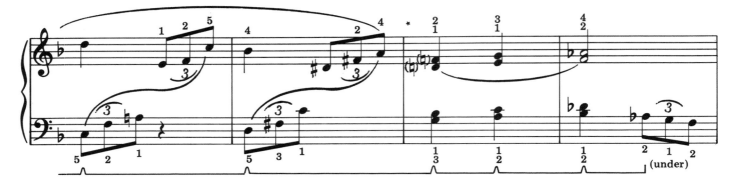

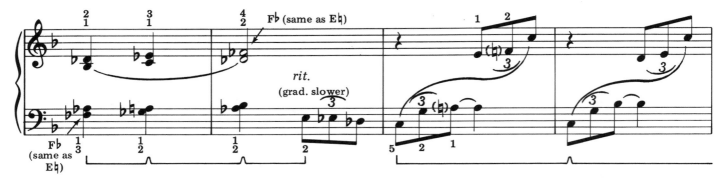

Hold all notes down with pedal for sustaining effect

* Courtesy Accidental

REMINDER that accidentals of previous bar (measure) were for that measure only. **ACCIDENTALS DO NOT CROSS THE BAR LINE.**

THE I, IV AND V CHORDS

The three most important basic **CHORDS** ARE FORMED STARTING ON THE 1st, 4th and 5th notes of the Major Scale. Using Roman Numerals they are called:

The **I CHORD** = **TONIC** (Major Triad)

The **IV CHORD** = **SUB-DOMINANT** (a Major Triad based on the **KEY** of the new starting note — the **4th** note)

The **V CHORD** = **DOMINANT** (a Major Triad based on the **KEY** of the new starting note - the **5th** note)

Key of C Major (Major Scale)

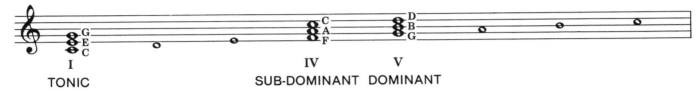

Thusly, the **IV CHORD** of C Major is the same as the **I CHORD** of F Major;
the **V CHORD** of C Major is the same as the **I CHORD** of G Major, etc.

A new Major Triad is built from each new starting note, in relation to the Major Scale Pattern of the **KEY** of that new note. The new note becomes the first note (1) of the new Major Scale. In the **Key of F Major** you would have the 1st, 3rd and 5th notes of **THAT** scale, or the notes of F A C., in the **Key of G Major**, the 1st, 3rd and 5th notes would be G B D., etc.

(MAJOR SCALE PATTERN)

Key of F Major
(B♭ signature)

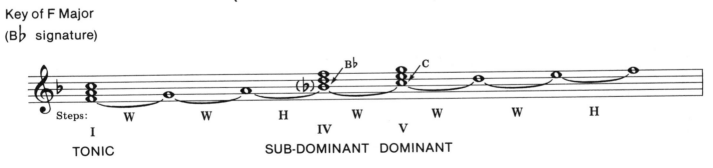

Accordingly, in the Key of F Major we have a new set of Major Triads, built on the 1st, 4th and 5th notes (I, IV, V) of the Major Scale Pattern of **THAT** Key.

The I Chord is based on 1, 3 & 5 of the **Key of F Major** . . .
The IV Chord **STARTS** on a B♭ in this case, so you would build a Major Triad of notes 1, 3 & 5 of the **Key of B♭** . . .
The V Chord **STARTS** on a **C**, therefore we build a Major Triad of 1, 3 & 5 notes of the **Key of C Major.**

REMEMBER THE MAJOR SCALE PATTERN IS THE SAME FOR *ALL* KEYS!

A CHORD IN SEARCH OF A MELODY

By MATT DENNIS a.s.c.a.p.

PASSING NOTE: A melodic note passing between notes of a chord.

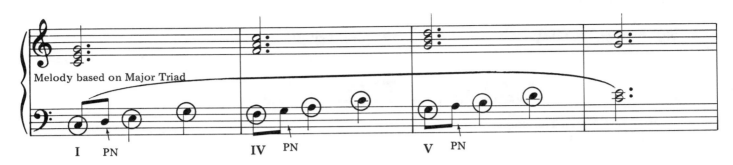

Inversions of the Major Triad, for reading and playing convenience.

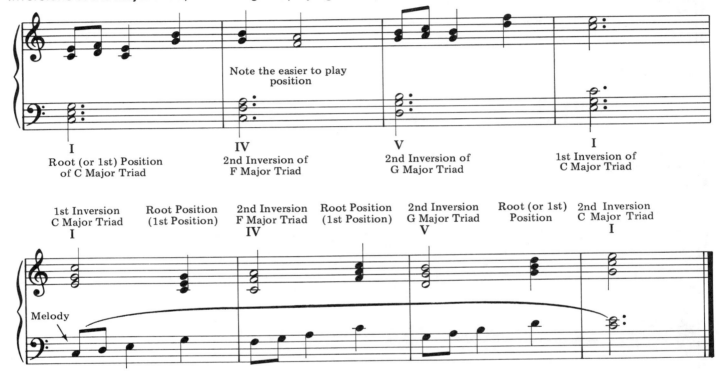

CHORD INVERSIONS IN THREE MAJOR KEYS

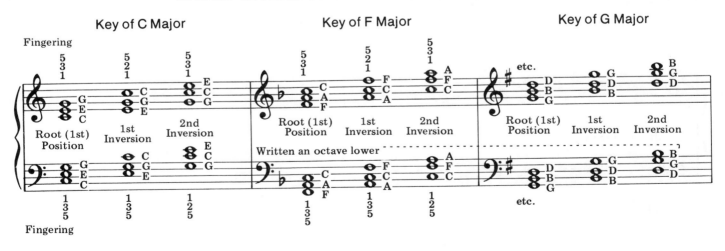

FOR AN ORIGINAL SET OF INTERESTING CHORD-FINGER EXERCISES, PLEASE TURN TO THE SPECIAL SECTION "FEELING THE CHORDS."

KEY OF B♭ MAJOR

Signature - Two flats, B♭ and E♭ 　　 B♭ Major Scale Pattern

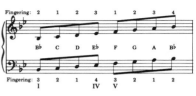

SALUTE THE MAJOR

Moderate March Tempo

By MATT DENNIS a.s.c.a.p.

THE TRADITIONAL BLUES FORMULA used the **I, IV** and **V CHORDS,** and was 12 Bars in length. As the **BLUES** form became more popular, new, more modern chord harmonies were introduced, expanding the improvisation possibilities. We shall have examples of **MODERN BLUES,** shortly, as we get into **SYNCOPATION** and **CONTEMPORARY CHORDS. HERE IS A BLUES WITH THE 3 CHORD FORMULA:**

ORIGINAL BLUES IN B♭
(THE 12 BAR BLUES)

Moderately Slow—Steady 4 Beat Tempo

By MATT DENNIS a.s.c.a.p.

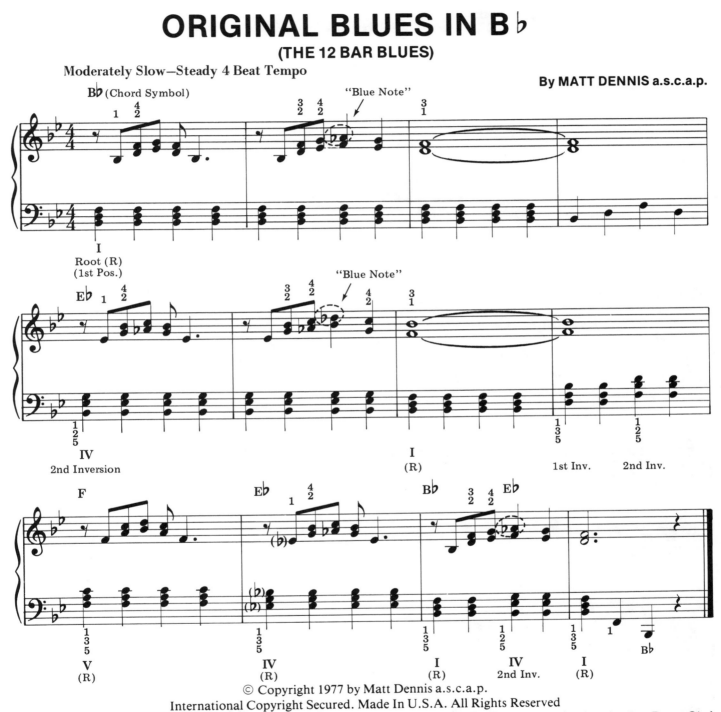

CHORD SYMBOLS = Names of the fundamental **CHORDS** used in each measure, whether in the Bass Clef, Treble Clef (in the Melodic structure), or in a combination of the notes in **BOTH** Clefs. You will run across this in most **POPULAR MUSIC.** Some pianists, *with a full knowledge of CHORD HARMONIES,* can read a Melody from the Sheet Music and play the proper harmony with interesting *inversions* of the **CHORDS,** just by reading the **CHORD SYMBOLS.** Your playing can have more individual style when you do this . . . it is an enjoyable experience and certainly a worthwhile goal. **BECOME FAMILIAR WITH CHORD INVERSIONS IN VARIOUS KEYS.**

"BLUE NOTE" = "Flatted" notes, characteristic of "The Blues."

SIXTEENTH (16th) NOTES

$\sqcap$ = ♩ a Quarter Note

$\sqcap$ = ♪ an 8th note

♬ = Half the value of an 8th note

A 16th rest ♯ = Half the value of an 8th rest

THE RACE IS ON

Allegro (Lively)

By MATT DENNIS a.s.c.a.p.

Count: 1 - e - an - da 2 - e - an - da   etc.

Count: (1) e - an - da 2 - e - an - da   etc.

(1) e - an - da 2 - e - an - da   etc.

16th rest

16th rest

KEY OF D MAJOR

Signature - Two sharps, F# and C#

D Major Scale Pattern

TURKEY IN THE STRAUSS

By **MATT DENNIS** a.s.c.a.p.

Moderate Waltz

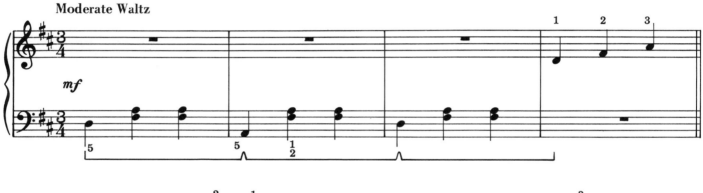

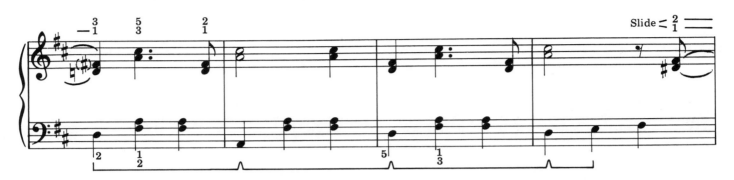

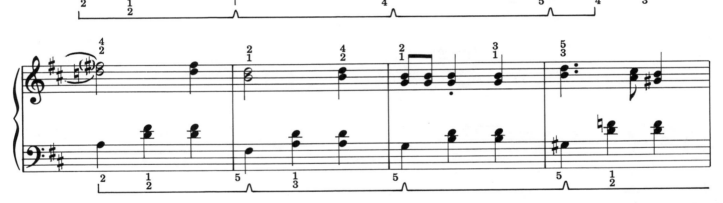

PANORAMA

Key of D Major
Signature - F♯ and C♯

Composed and Arranged By
MATT DENNIS a.s.c.a.p.

Andante—with expression

TERMS:

Andante = Moderately slow
poco accel. = Slightly faster
    poco = A little, slight
    accel. (accelerando) = Becoming faster
rall. (rallentando) means same as "rit." = Gradually slower
a tempo = return to original tempo

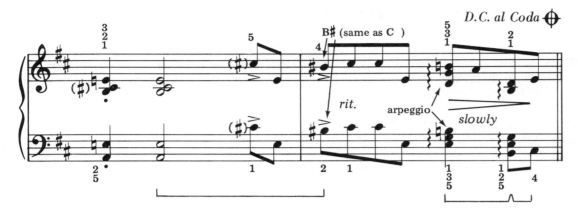

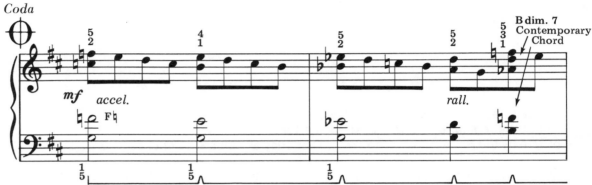

OBSERVE the many new things to learn and remember in the above piece, such as:

ARPEGGIO = A "Broken Chord" starting with the lowest note in the L.H., ending up with the top note in the R.H. The Chord has a "harp-like" effect when played with the Damper Pedal held down.

accel. = accelerando, or play gradually faster

rall. = rallentando, or play gradually slower . . . same meaning as rit. or ritardando.

CONTEMPORARY CHORDS = Interesting sounding Modern Chords. See notes under **"FEELING THE CHORDS"** at end of this book, regarding study of such Chords.

AND NOW, a most important **RHYTHM STUDY** called

SYNCOPATION

Originating in early **RAGTIME MUSIC** (Scott Joplin, etc.), **SYNCOPATION** became the driving force of **BLUES,** then **JAZZ,** and finally a vital and commonly accepted part of all **POPULAR MUSIC.** It will take some concentration at first, to master the feeling of **SYNCOPATION,** but *once you've got the beat, you'll never forget it . . . it's infectious!*

SYNCOPATION may be generally defined as the catchy, unexpected "off-beat" rhythm caused by *shifting the accent to the* **WEAK** *beats of a measure, and holding through the* **STRONG** *beats, for example*

In 4/4 Time, the *regular beats* in a measure are

1	**2**	**3**	**4**
STRONG	**WEAK**	**MED. STRONG**	**WEAK**
beat	**beat**	**beat**	**beat**

Syncopated notes are *circled* in the following exercises

1. The simplest form of **SYNCOPATION** and easiest to understand . . .
   Count the *regular beats* as played by the Left Hand in the Bass Clef, and you will feel the *syncopated beats* played by the Right Hand in the Treble Clef. Play at a steady tempo.

   The *accented* 2nd beat in the Right Hand now becomes a **STRONG** beat, and the 3rd beat becomes what we call a *silent* beat, since the note is being held through that beat.

AS WRITTEN:

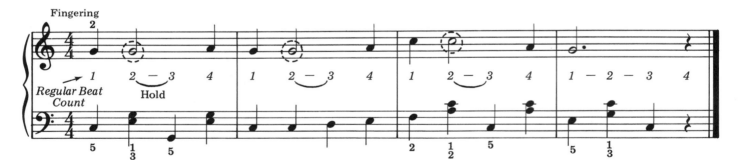

SOUNDS SAME AS:

2. Another familiar pattern of **SYNCOPATION...**
   Again, notes are played *just ahead of, in anticipation of, a regular beat, and held through all or part of that beat — in some cases, the notes held may be* **TIED** *to the next beat or beats.*

   Observe, in *Treble Clef* measures 1 and 3, the first half of the 4th beat is *silent,* as you are holding a note through that part of the beat. Likewise, in measures 1, 2 and 3 you are playing an eighth note on the last half of the 4th beat, which is **TIED** *to following notes and beats.* These beats, held and counted but not played, are called *silent* beats.

AS WRITTEN:

SOUNDS SAME AS:

3. Same rhythm pattern as above, only for *Left Hand in the Bass Clef . . .*
   Count the *regular beats,* and play steadily.

AS WRITTEN:

SOUNDS SAME AS:

MORE SYNCOPATION in the following **FOUR PIANO PIECES**, covering

BLUES, RAGTIME, JAZZ and POP (Popular) PIANO STYLES

Play over each piece several times, counting the *regular beats,* and observe how the syncopated (accented) notes are played *just ahead of the next regular beat,* etc. **SYNCOPATION** can occur in different parts of a measure, as there are many patterns. *Keep the tempo steady* and eventually you should get the *feeling* of syncopated rhythm.

THE BLUES . . . usually a sad, mournful melody with simple harmony and a *beat*

LONESOME MORNIN' BLUES

By MATT DENNIS a.s.c.a.p.

Chord Syncopation

© Copyright 1977 by Matt Dennis a.s.c.a.p.
International Copyright Secured. Made In U.S.A. All Rights Reserved

NOTE: When the **BEAT** is fairly established in the R.H. Melody, by the Syncopated notation, the L.H. can play a sustained Interval or chord accompaniment (as above). Just be sure to keep the *regular beat count* going steadily.

70

RAGTIME . . . a lively, old fashioned melody with a syncopated beat

"NICKELODEON":

The name for the early Silent Movie Theatre, where admission was a **NICKEL.**

RAGTIME and Melodramatic Music was the accompaniment to such movies, played "live" by a pianist or organist. This particular sound became so popular it was carried over into the era of the newly invented Player Piano, as leading pianists made *piano rolls* playing Ragtime, Blues, Jazz, Classical Themes and the current Popular Songs.

Great composers such as Debussy, Ravel, Ellington, Gershwin, etc. made early piano rolls which have become rare collectors' items.

Soon, the *Mechanical* Player Piano was invented . . . put a **NICKEL** in the slot and you would hear the piano roll of your choice, while you enjoyed watching the keys go up and down, mysteriously, with no one at the keyboard. The resulting happy, jazzy, fun sound became known as **NICKELODEON MUSIC.**

Thanks to the influence of the fine music of such as Scott Joplin, Ragtime, Player Piano and **NICKELODEON MUSIC** all seem to be enjoying as much popularity today as ever. New piano rolls are being made of the latest top Pop Songs, and the old favorites are always in demand, reminding us of this colorful period of our musical culture.

NICKELODEON RAG
(AUTHENTIC STYLE)

By MATT DENNIS a.s.c.a.p.

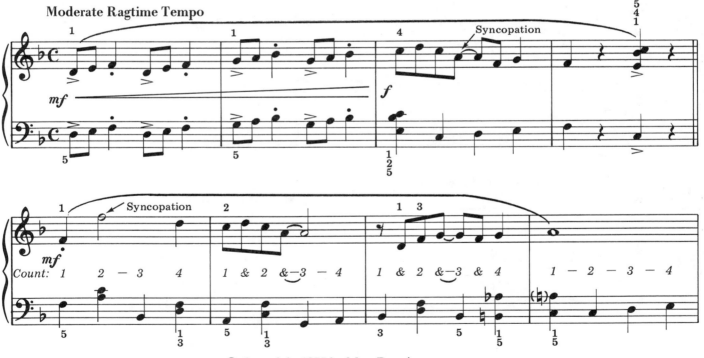

REMINDER:

    ACCENT   = Strong touch

    STACCATO = **dot** *over or under* a note, let note up quickly, short touch

JAZZ ... AN AMERICAN TRADITION, with roots in **BLUES** and **RAGTIME.**
A more sophisticated form of music with syncopated rhythms and freely improvised melodies and chord harmonies ... completely Contemporary in style. Always open to the latest imaginative ideas of the instrumental player, **JAZZ MOVES WITH THE TIMES.**

The **JAZZ PIANO PIECE** below, will give you an idea of this exciting form. It shows the *Right Hand Melody* played in a *syncopated* rhythm, against the *Left Hand Regular Bass Pattern* (in 4/4 time). You will find it **EASY TO PLAY,** by counting the beats evenly. Note the syncopation played by *both hands* in the final measures. *Dotted lines* indicate where the *syncopated notes* are to be played *between regular beats.*

ALONG CAME JAZZ

By MATT DENNIS a.s.c.a.p.

NOTE use of **STACCATO** and **ACCENT MARKS.**

NOTE use of **CHORDS** (3 or more notes played together) in last 4 measures (bars). Different **INTERVALS** (2 notes) in each hand or clef, when played together form a **CHORD**. The **INTERVAL** in the L.H. when added to the 3 note **CHORD** in the R.H. will form a more complete sounding **CHORD**.

This is called **CHORD VOICING** and the particular **CHORD HARMONY** used above is **CONTEMPORARY,** or close sounding. *See Supplemental Study by* **MATT DENNIS "CONTEMPORARY CHORDS and CHORD VOICING"** *for full explanations and examples.*

JAZZ is not only a medium for original composition, but many of the best known **POPULAR SONGS** *of all time* have become "Standards," and will remain so due to the **JAZZ** treatment given them by top professional singers and musicians in live and recorded performances. The **POP SONG OF TODAY,** as well as the **POP ARTIST,** is greatly influenced by **JAZZ.**

Your author, as a well recognized **JAZZ** and **POP SONG** Composer-Pianist, can vouch for the above statement, since many of his original songs have become "Standards," thanks to the creative efforts of fine **JAZZ** artists, many of whom are world famous. (Songs such as: **ANGEL EYES, LET'S GET AWAY FROM IT ALL, VIOLETS FOR YOUR FURS, EVERYTHING HAPPENS TO ME, etc.**).

POPULAR MUSIC — THE POPULAR SONG . . .

A combination of a **MELODY** (with or without lyrics), and **PIANO ACCOMPANIMENT.** May be in many moods and styles, such as **BLUES, RAGTIME, JAZZ, FOLK, COUNTRY, SPIRITUAL, ROCK, BROADWAY THEATRE, MOVIE & TV THEMES,** etc. Usually, either a **BALLAD** (slow tempo) or a **RHYTHM** piece (faster tempo), the latter being somewhat *syncopated.*

Think of syncopated notes as *Push Beats,* or notes played just ahead of regular beats, and play these notes with a relaxed feeling, not stiffly.

BELOW . . . we have an easy to play example of a typical **POP** (Popular) **SONG,** as arranged in **SHEET MUSIC** form, with a **VOICE** line (Melody) for the singer to follow, and the **PIANO ACCOMPANIMENT** part. While some piano parts are written *without* the Melody included, to be played as a strict accompaniment to a singer, the *best* arrangement for piano will *include* the Melody so that the song may be played in complete form as a piano solo.

JUST THE WAY YOU LOOK

Lyric and Music by
MATT DENNIS a.s.c.a.p.

OBSERVE special footnotes at end of piece.

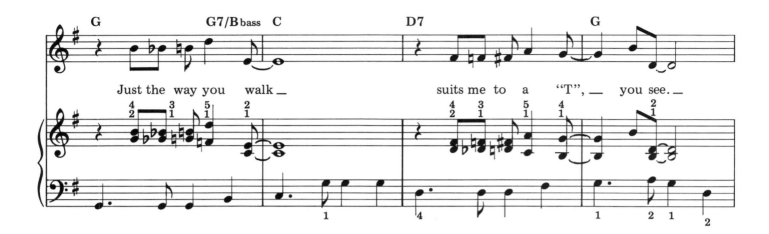

Just the way you walk _ suits me to a "T", _ you see. _

Love the way you talk, _ love the way you look. _

_ Fun-ny, but ev - 'ry time when I am near to you, sud-den-ly my heart soars up to the

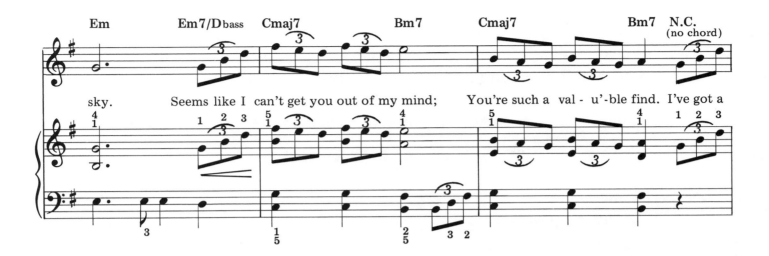

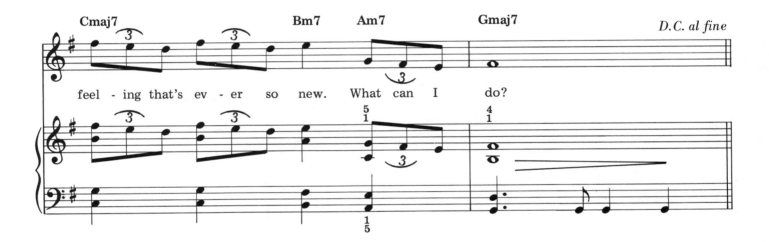

FINGERING is added to the above piece as a convenience only, since this is not the usual procedure in most **POP SHEET MUSIC.**

CHORD SYMBOLS such as the **G, C, D,** etc., are placed above the **VOICE** line just to give you an idea of the looks of the professional sheet music arrangement. We shall be getting into these and more advanced **CHORDS** IN OUR STUDIES AND PIECES TO FOLLOW.

Guitar Chord Diagrams are usually shown, also, just below the **CHORD SYMBOLS,** — however since we are primarily dealing with **PIANO,** in this case they are not necessary.

D.C. al fine: go back to beginning and play to end ("fine").

ACCENT SIGNS (Over or under a note)

(marcato) = strike note harder, louder

(staccato) = strike note with short crisp attack, then let up

(tenuto) = strike note firmly, hold for full value (opposite of staccato)

TOGETHERNESS

By MATT DENNIS a.s.c.a.p.

Moderately, with a lilt

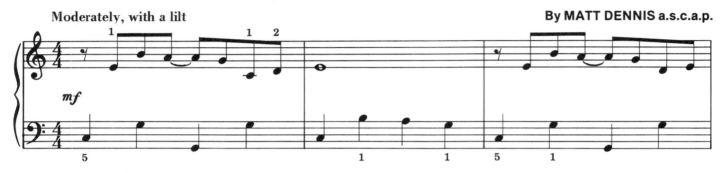

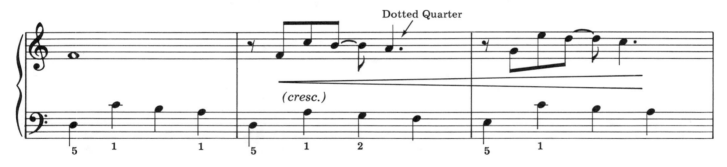

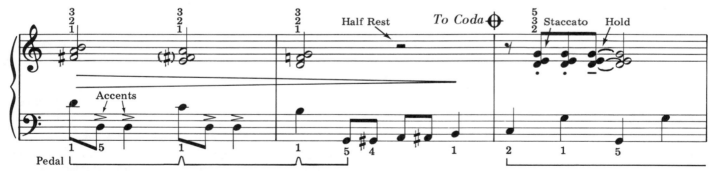

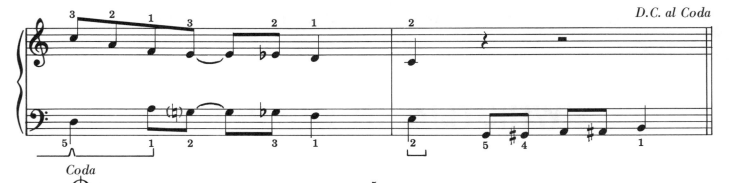

D.C. al Coda

Coda

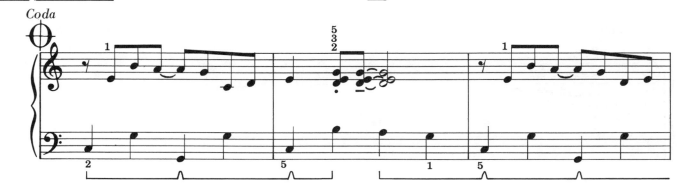

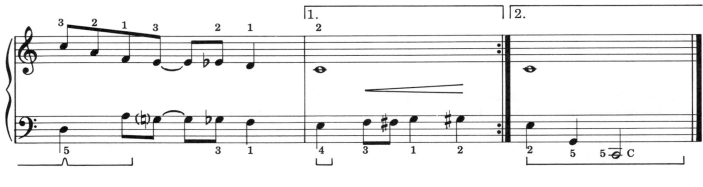

DOTTED EIGHTH AND SIXTEENTH NOTES

TOGETHER ♩. ♪ = 1 BEAT

THIS RHYTHMIC NOTATION IS COMMONLY USED IN POPULAR MUSIC.
OBSERVE we are using **INNER LEDGER LINE NOTES** with the L.H.

WHISTLIN' IN THE PARK

By MATT DENNIS a.s.c.a.p.

¢ = "CUT TIME" OR 2/2 TIME (HALF NOTE GETS ONE BEAT)
Learn to play in 4/4 then pick up tempo and count 2 Beats to a measure.

NOTE: L.H. moves up into the Treble Clef and back to Bass Clef in measures 5 & 6, then up again in measures 13 through 16.

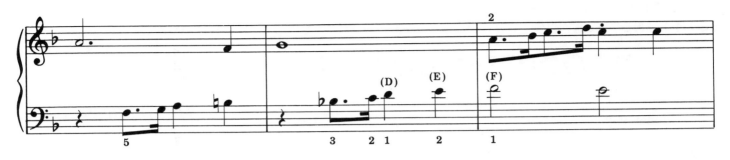

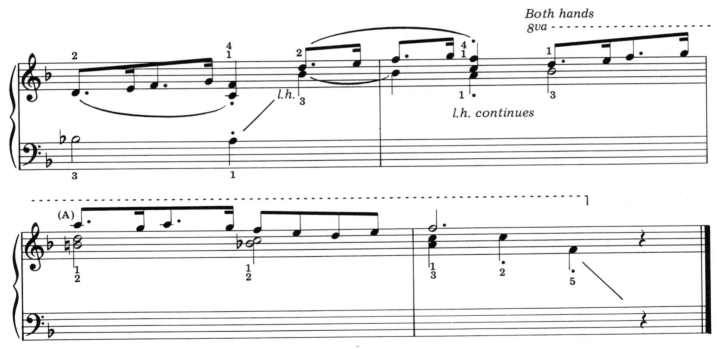

8va . . . .

PLAY NOTES UNDER THIS SIGN AN OCTAVE (8 NOTES) HIGHER THAN WRITTEN.
In the example above, **BOTH HANDS** are played in this manner.

Should this sign appear **BELOW** notes of the **BASS CLEF,** this means such notes are to be played **AN OCTAVE** (8 notes) **LOWER** than written.

THE EXCITING AND VERY POPULAR BOOGIE WOOGIE RHYTHM.
BOTH HANDS PLAYING "DOTTED 8TH & 16TH NOTES" WITH A STEADY BEAT

BOOGIE WOOGIE ON THE BLUES

By MATT DENNIS a.s.c.a.p.

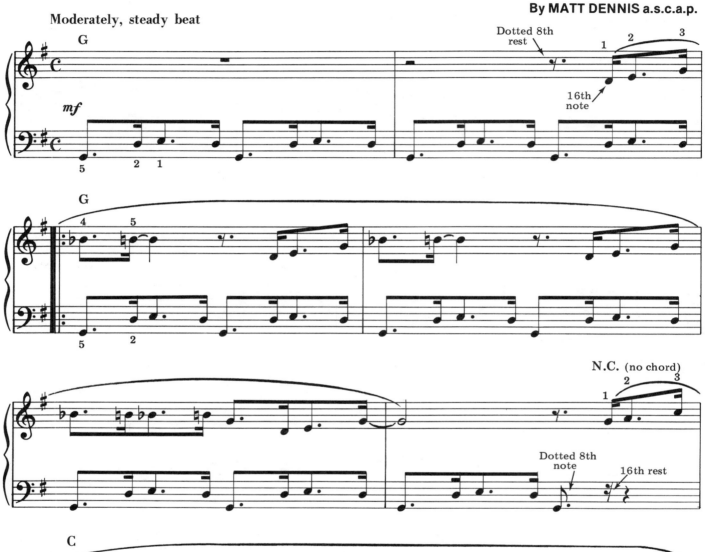

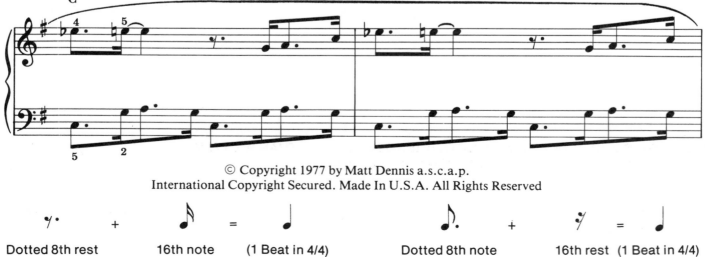

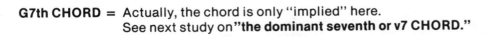

G7th CHORD = Actually, the chord is only "implied" here.
See next study on **"the dominant seventh or v7 CHORD."**

INTRODUCING

THE DOMINANT SEVENTH

OR V7 CHORD

THE DOMINANT SEVENTH or **V7 CHORD** is an extension of the regular **DOMINANT** or **V CHORD** we learned about in the study of **THE MAJOR SCALE PATTERN** and the **I, IV** and **V CHORDS.**

To the **DOMINANT MAJOR TRIAD, ADD** note **THREE HALF STEPS** above. This is the **"FLATTED SEVENTH"** note of **THAT** particular Key. See example below.

THIS CHORD, discovered through the early improvisational playing of **THE BLUES,** is commonly used in **POPULAR MUSIC,** and the first of many interesting ones we shall experience.

Keep in mind that **ALL CHORDS** and harmonic inventions are based on the **I, IV** and **V CHORDS** . . . notes may be added or altered, to create the more involved or sophisticated **CHORD SOUNDS,** making the harmonies richer and more exciting to the ear and more enjoyable to play on the **PIANO.**

In Relation to the
Key of C Major

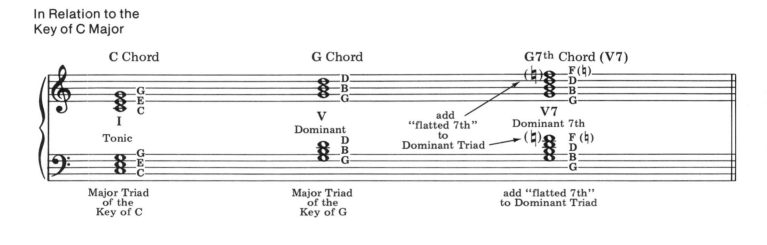

INVERSIONS OF THE V7 CHORD

There are FOUR Positions of this chord

Key of C Major

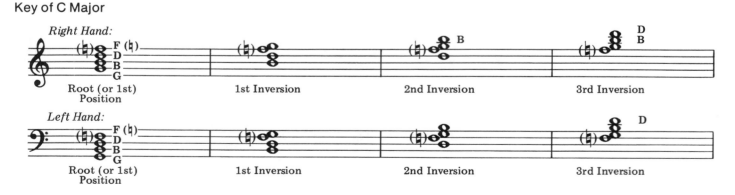

LIKEWISE, in the **KEY OF F MAJOR** the **V7 CHORD** would be built on the 5th note of **THAT** scale pattern, etc., etc. . . *the rule applies to ALL Keys.*

In relation to the
Key of F Major

THE FIVE-SEVEN BLUES
(V7)

By MATT DENNIS a.s.c.a.p.

IN THE EARLY THREE CHORD BLUES FORMULA . . . the **I, IV** and **V CHORDS** were used. Musicians found that the **V7** was a more musical **CHORD** and this has been used to replace the **V CHORD** in most cases. See the **NINTH MEASURE,** above.

KEY OF E♭ MAJOR

Signature - Three flats, B♭ - E♭ - A♭

E♭ MAJOR SCALE PATTERN

THE DREAM

Key of E♭ Major

By MATT DENNIS a.s.c.a.p.

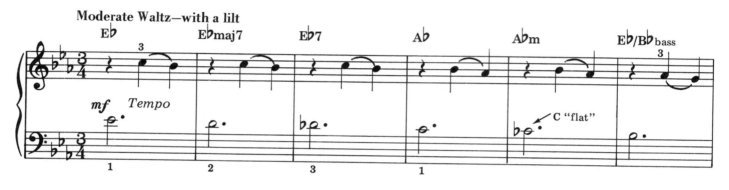

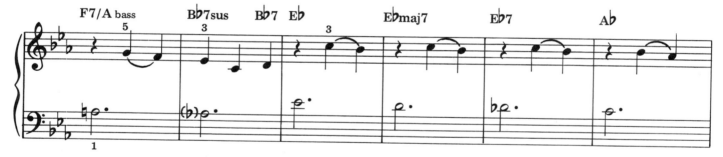

CHORD SYMBOLS throughout the selection are indicated only as a guide to show you the pattern of harmony **IMPLIED** by the movement of the notation. You will not be playing any Chords, with the exception of Measures 17 - 28, where the harmony is more spelled out in the *voicing* of the Chords.

Chords such as A♭m, Am7 and B♭m7 have to do with the **MINOR CHORDS.** We shall have examples of such **CHORDS** in our study of **THE MINOR KEY AND CHORDS,** shortly.

When you see a **CHORD** like the E♭/B♭ Bass, etc., this simply means the B♭ is the best **LEADING** note at that point, and moves more naturally to the next Bass note in the pattern. This is called **VOICE LEADING.**

The **CHORDS** in brackets (Am7), (D7), etc., as in the 4 measures leading up to the "D.C. al fine sign", are **implied chords** for the musical phrase they cover, and are not meant to be played, as you can see by the simple notation.

A SONG OF FAITH

MESSENGER OF LOVE
(SPIRITUAL)

Key of E♭ Major

By MATT DENNIS a.s.c.a.p.

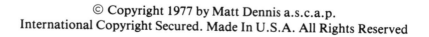

KEY OF A MAJOR

Signature - Three Sharps, F♯ - C♯ - G♯

POLKA DOT POLKA

A STUDY IN *THIRDS* —
PLAYING IN TWO KEYS:
Key of A Major & Key of D Major

By MATT DENNIS a.s.c.a.p.

THIRDS = INTERVALS of a **THIRD,** two notes played with the **FINGERS** 1 - 3, 2 - 4 & 3 - 5, and in reverse order, as in above piece. Great exercise for flexibility of the fingers.

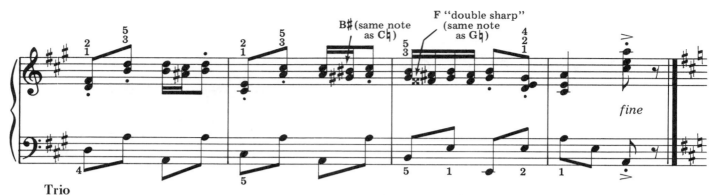

Trio
Key of D Major

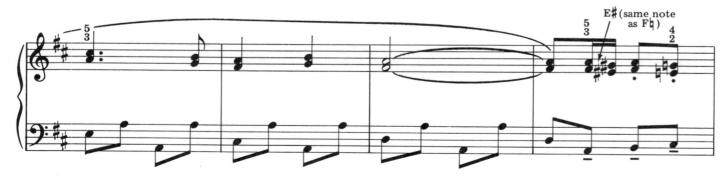

✗ = **"DOUBLE SHARP" SIGN** . . . raise or "sharp" the note another half step . . . The F♯ (above) would be raised another half step, so you would play the note of **G.**

D.C. al fine

THE POLKA...

A most enthusiastic Dance Form, Bohemian in origin from the 19th Century, and very popular today. The Music is Jolly and suggests Happy Times.   *M.D.*

SIGHT READING POPULAR MUSIC
VOICE LINES

Each line of music is called a **VOICE,** very much like a Singer's Voice, and the notes of any line add up to the time value, in each measure, indicated by the Time Signature of a piece.

The **MELODY** alone would be **ONE VOICE,** but we are concerned with **TWO, THREE** or **FOUR VOICE** patterns, to take care of accompaniment and harmonization of the Melody. To understand the function of such **VOICE** lines, compare to the **VOICES** of a **SOLOIST, DUO, TRIO** or **QUARTET** of Singers. The average **POP** piece will use a *combination* of **VOICE** lines.

A. **TWO VOICE** pattern . . . Most Popular . . . basic and easiest to read and play

      1st Voice: Right Hand plays the Melody in the Treble Clef, solo, or with added harmony
      2nd Voice: Left Hand plays the Bass accompaniment in the Bass Clef

Note that **BOTH VOICES** receive an **EQUAL** amount of **BEATS** per measure, as indicated by the Time Signature (4/4 in example below).

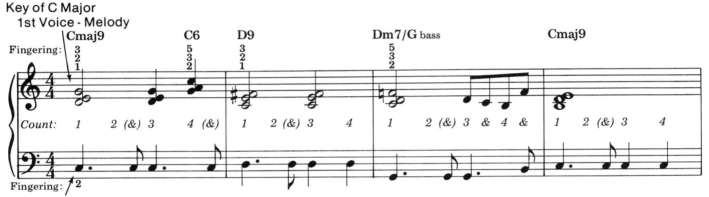

B. **THREE VOICE** pattern . . . Next Most Popular, as it allows for more harmony and rhythm accompaniment, with the divided fingers of the Right Hand

      1st Voice: R.H. plays the Melody with **UPPER** fingers of the hand
      2nd Voice: R.H. plays harmony or rhythm accompaniment with the **LOWER** fingers.
      3rd Voice: L.H. plays the Bass accompaniment.

ALL VOICES receive **EQUAL** amount of **BEATS** per measure, per Time Signature.

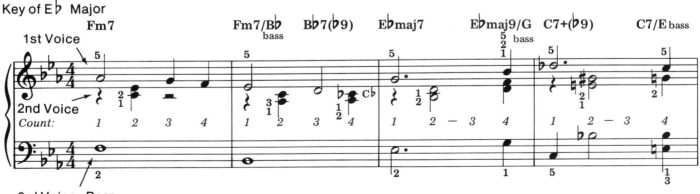

CHORD SYMBOLS used are just to represent a typical **POP** sheet music arrangement. For **CHORD** study see notes under **"FEELING THE CHORDS."**

C. **FOUR VOICE** pattern . . . More difficult, but interesting as it provides a more complete harmonic and rhythmic accompaniment to a Melody.

      1st Voice: Right Hand plays the Melody with **UPPER** fingers of the hand
      2nd Voice: R.H. plays harmony or rhythm accompaniment with **LOWER** fingers
      3rd Voice: Left Hand plays additional harmony or rhythm accompaniment with **UPPER** fingers of L.H.
      4th Voice: L.H. plays the fundamental Bass notes with **LOWER** fingers.

(1.) **ALL VOICES** receive **EQUAL** amount of **BEATS** per measure, as indicated by Time Signature.

Key of C Major

1st Voice - Melody
2nd Voice - Accompaniment

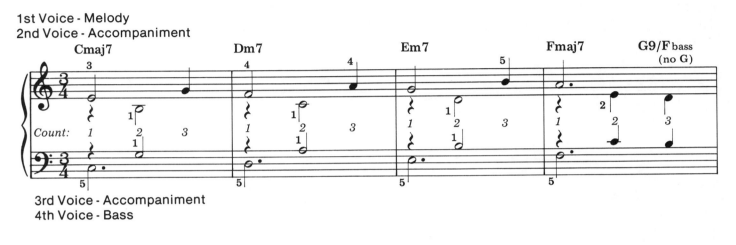

3rd Voice - Accompaniment
4th Voice - Bass

The **STEMS** of the notes go **UP** or **DOWN** depending on the **VOICE** lines the notes are following. You may **PLAY AND HOLD** A NOTE WHILE YOU PLAY ANOTHER NOTE. Each **VOICE** has its separate **COUNT** of **BEATS**.

(2.) **ANOTHER EXAMPLE OF THE FOUR VOICE PATTERN,** in **4/4 TIME** with Syncopation.

Key of G Major

1st Voice - Melody
2nd Voice - Accompaniment (harmony)

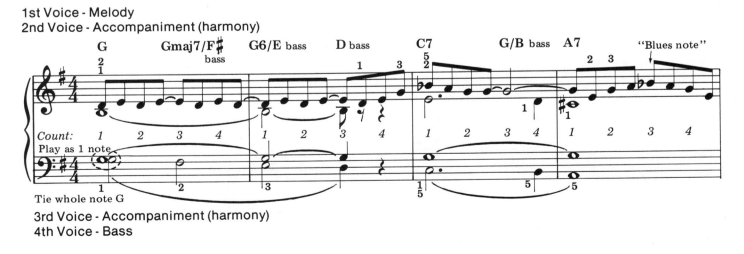

3rd Voice - Accompaniment (harmony)
4th Voice - Bass

For excellent practice, examine sheet music you may have at hand, and notice the different **VOICE** lines of each selection. Recognize and play the lines.

93

This selection shows the simple use of
TWO VOICE and **FOUR VOICE** lines
in an easy to play and understand
piano arrangement.

ONE FINE DAY

By MATT DENNIS a.s.c.a.p.

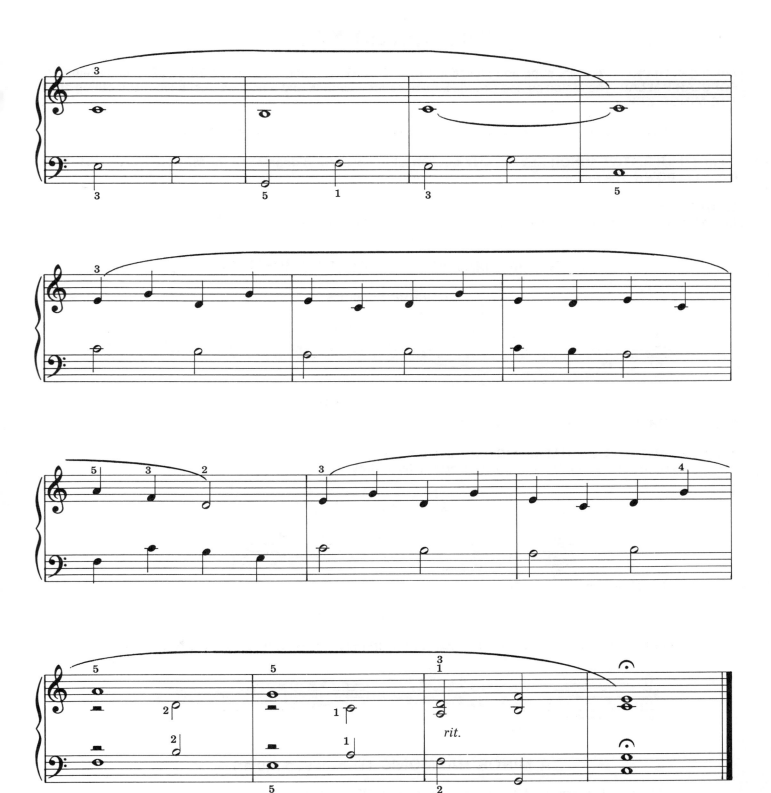

THE MINOR KEY

Much great music is written, sung and played in the **MINOR KEYS,** such as **THE BLUES, JAZZ,** and certainly the **POPULAR BALLAD.** The Melodies and Chord Harmonies are haunting and emotional. Let's learn something about **THE MINOR KEY.**

EVERY MAJOR KEY HAS A RELATIVE MINOR KEY . . . using the same Major Key Signature.

To find the **RELATIVE MINOR KEY OF ANY MAJOR KEY,** count **UP** 6 degrees of the **MAJOR SCALE PATTERN, OR** count **DOWN** 3 half-steps.

EXAMPLE:
In the Key of **C MAJOR** the note being **"A"** puts us in the **RELATIVE** Key of **A MINOR.**

KEY OF C MAJOR   RELATIVE MINOR "A"

Count **UP** 6 degrees

or Count **DOWN** 3 half steps

There are **THREE** varieties of the **MINOR SCALE**

NATURAL, MELODIC, and **HARMONIC** (the most popular)
They all have the same Key Signature as the relative Major Key.

A MINOR NATURAL

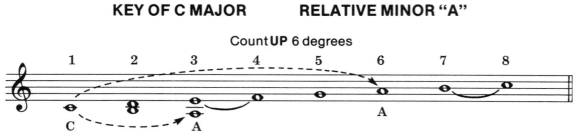

Chord Pattern: I   IV   V

A MINOR MELODIC

The 6th & 7th degrees are raised ½ step, going **UP** only. . Coming **DOWN,** they become natural.

A MINOR HARMONIC (The most popular)

The 7th degree **ONLY** is raised ½ step, both **UP** and **DOWN.**
This is a most musical scale and has an exotic sound.

THE MINOR KEYS

The Relative Minor Key of the Key of C Major being the Key of A Minor, then, for the following Keys here are their relative Minor Keys:

F Major (B♭ Sig.)	- D Minor
G Major (F♯ Sig.)	- E Minor
B♭ Major (B♭, E♭)	- G Minor
D Major (F♯, C♯)	- B Minor
E♭ Major (B♭, E♭, A♭)	- C Minor

*PRACTICE EXERCISE . . . work out the relative **MINOR KEY SCALES** for each of the Major Keys listed, keeping in mind the **MINOR KEY SCALES** have the *same* **KEY SIGNATURES** as their relative Major Keys.

THE MINOR KEY CHORDS

THE MINOR KEY has its own **I, IV** and **V CHORD PATTERN,** consisting of **TWO MINOR CHORDS** and **ONE MAJOR CHORD,**

THE 3 BASIC MINOR TRIADS (CHORDS)			THE MINOR SEVENTH	THE DOMINANT SEVENTH
(I)	(IV)	(V)	(m7)	(V7)

EXAMPLE: KEY OF A MINOR (Relative to Key of C Major)

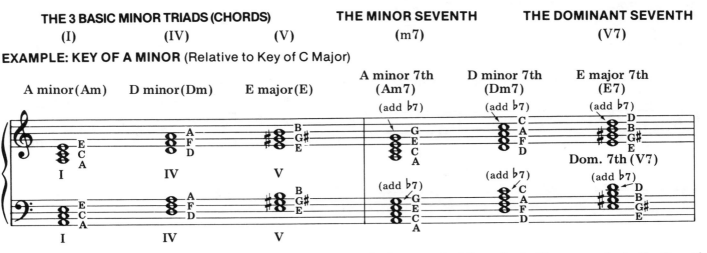

BASIC MINOR TRIADS: The Minor Triads are built on the 1 - 3 - 5 notes of a Minor Scale. For example, in the Key of **A MINOR,** the notes are A - C - E.

THE MINOR SEVENTH CHORD: To the *Minor* Triad **ADD "THE NATURAL SEVENTH"** or note 1½ steps above the 5th note of the Triad. (1½ steps = 3 half steps)

DOMINANT SEVENTH CHORD: As we learned previously, to the **MAJOR** Triad **ADD "THE FLATTED SEVENTH"** or note 1½ steps above the 5th note of the Triad. This is the **V7** Chord.

SAME CHORDS — DIFFERENT KEY

EXAMPLE: KEY OF D MINOR (Relative to Key of F Major)

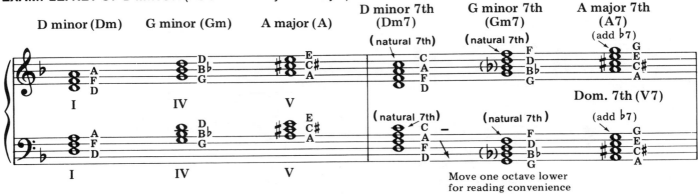

Move one octave lower
for reading convenience

FOR AN INTERESTING SET OF **MINOR KEY CHORD-FINGER EXERCISES** PLEASE TURN TO THE SPECIAL SECTION AT END OF THIS BOOK CALLED **"FEELING THE CHORDS."**

A NOVELTY PIECE IN A MINOR KEY

In this one selection we play and experience
- A Minor Key Melody,
- Minor Key Chords and Inversions,
- **TWO** Time Signatures in the same piece . . . 2/4 and 4/4,
- **PLUS** Special Chords

ALBERT'S GHOST

Key of A Minor

Allegro — Mysterioso

By MATT DENNIS a.s.c.a.p.

MYSTERIOSO: The suspenseful, mysterious sound created by the Minor Melody and Minor Chords, together with the steady tempo and special dynamics indicated.

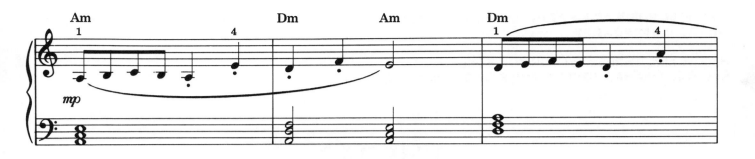

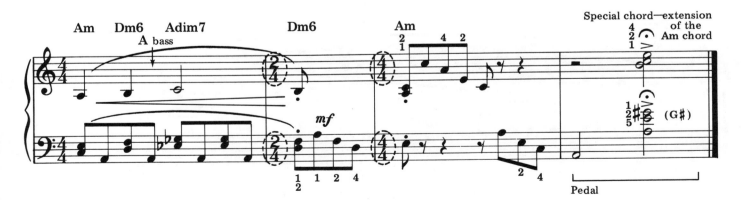

SPECIAL CHORD . . . We use such **CHORDS as the A Diminished 7th . . . so you might eventually become used to the fine modern harmonic sound they make, and be able to identify them by name.

A TYPICAL POPULAR PIECE can be written in a combination of **VOICE** lines. Test your Sight Reading with this **BALLAD** in a **MINOR KEY.**

Here we have **THREE** and **FOUR VOICE** lines.
Note use of the **HARMONIC MINOR SCALE** in the **MELODY.**

WHERE?

Key of D Minor
(Relative to Key of F Major)

By **MATT DENNIS a.s.c.a.p.**

*SPECIAL CHORDS . . . B♭7♭5 – play B♭ 7th and ♭5; A7 sus – play A 7th and add 4th, no 3rd, this resolves to the A 7th chord – with 3rd.
ARPEGGIO: Play in a "harp-like" fashion. . from bottom to top, as previously explained.

AUTHENTIC COUNTRY-WESTERN STYLE

using the popular dotted 8TH/16TH NOTE RHYTHM PATTERN

INTO THE SUNSET

By MATT DENNIS a.s.c.a.p.

Key of D Major

EVERYBODY'S FAVORITE IS THE PIANO THEME

Strongly emotional, melodic themes are used to dramatize important Motion Pictures, Stage and Television Productions. Some have been created from the Classics (Tchaikovsky, Debussy, etc.). Outstanding themes become immensely popular through the medium of Radio, TV and Recordings, and will usually feature the **PIANO,** supported by lush orchestral backgrounds.

Some memorable themes have been . . . **TONIGHT WE LOVE** (Tchaikovsky Piano Concerto), **TARA'S THEME** (Gone With The Wind), **TILL THE END OF TIME** (Chopin's Polinaise), **LARA'S THEME** (Dr. Zhivago), **THE SHADOW OF YOUR SMILE, LAURA, BORN FREE, THEME FROM LOVE STORY,** etc.

HERE IS AN ORIGINAL PIANO THEME, meant to convey some of the warmth and style of the above themes. Play the melody, the full harmonies and the steady Left Hand movement with expression. This was composed in the style of a Concerto.

INSPIRATION
(LOVE THEME)

Composed and Arranged by
MATT DENNIS a.s.c.a.p.

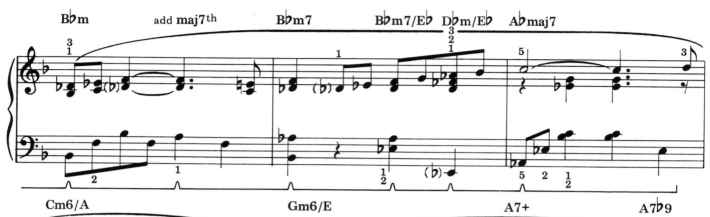

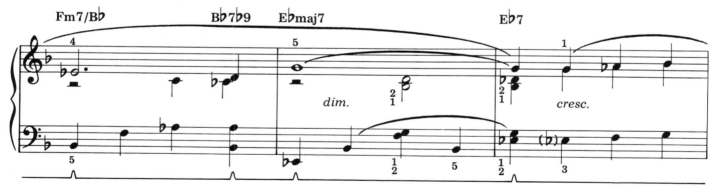

104

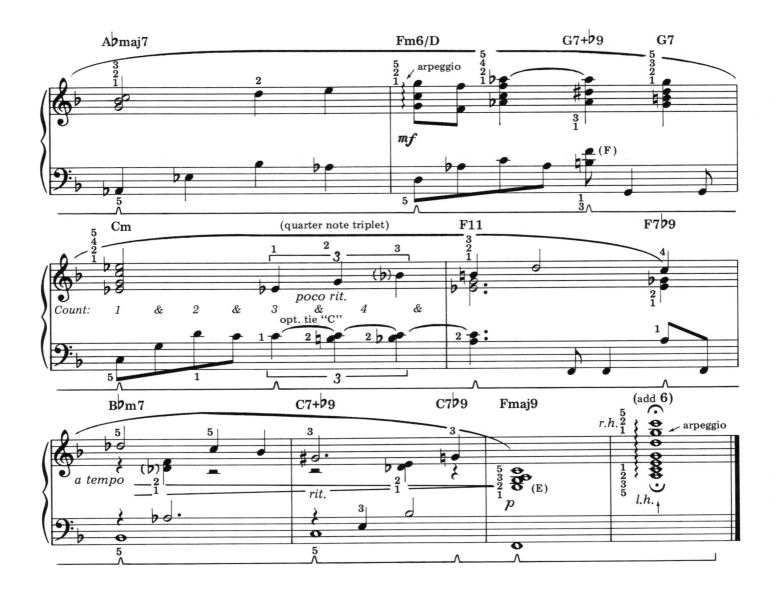

- ✔ You will notice we are using a combination of **TWO, THREE** and **FOUR VOICE LINES** in this selection.

- ✔ Observe the correct fingering in all cases, where suggested, to play with ease.

- ✔ **A TEMPO =** Return to the original tempo of the piece, after the slight slowing down in previous measures (poco rit.).

- ✔ Note use of the Arpeggio Chords in measures 26 and 32. Play in "harp-like" fashion, starting with bottom note in L.H., as defined previously. Octave chords are used in measures 26 and 27.

- ✔ **QUARTER NOTE TRIPLET =** **THREE** Quarter Notes joined with a bracket and the small numeral "3" . . . are played in the **TIME** of **TWO** Quarter Notes.

$$ \underbrace{\text{♩ ♩ ♩}}_{3} = \text{♩ ♩} \quad \text{or 2 beats} $$

As you will note in above measure 27, you must *wedge* the **THREE** Quarter Notes in the measure to the *TIME* of the 3rd and 4th beats, this is done more by **FEEL** than by count, **HOWEVER,** keep in mind *you must not slow down* to play the **THREE** notes, as you must keep the 4 beats per measure **CONSTANT.** This will become more natural as you have occasion to play the Quarter Note Triplet.

sight reading a pop-ROCK STYLED PIECE

Note the Major, Minor and Special Chords

SUMMER SCHOOL IN OXNARD

By MATT DENNIS a.s.c.a.p.

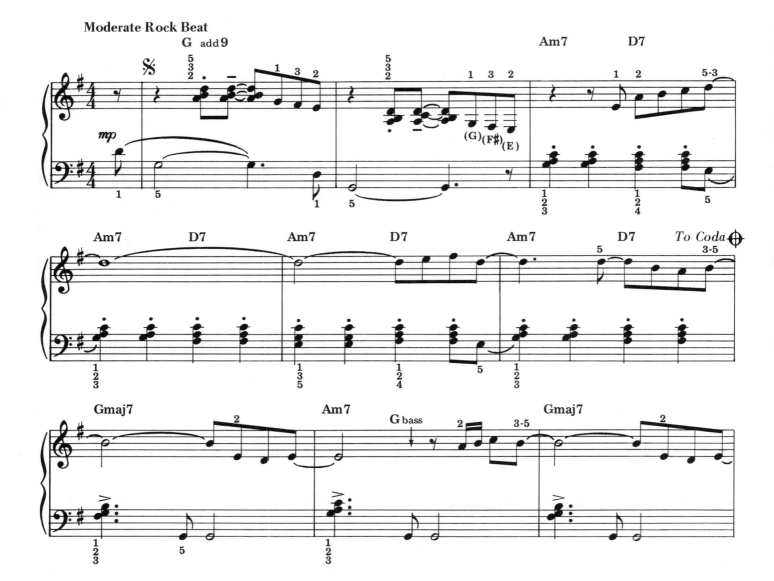

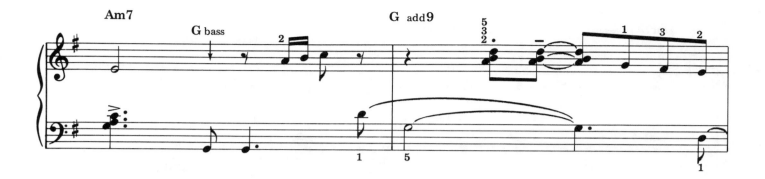

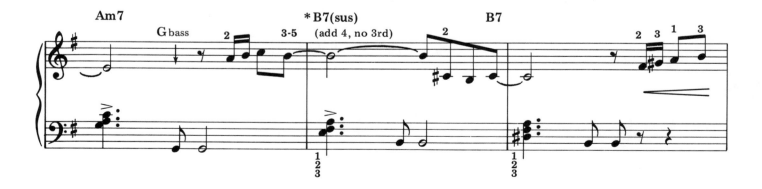

*SPECIAL CHORD —See "Feeling The Chords"—Page 109

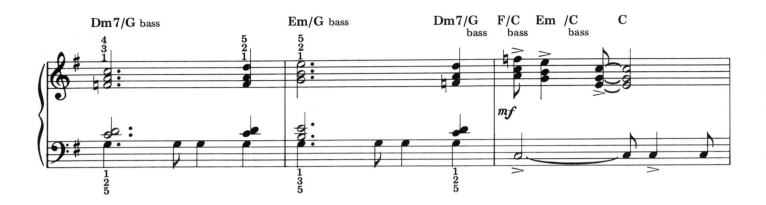

FEELING THE CHORDS

— MAJOR CHORDS WITH INVERSIONS —

CHORD - FINGER EXERCISES

The most natural way to play **CHORDS** with correct fingering and easiest form is to get the habit of **FEELING THE CHORDS**. The **CHORD EXERCISES** below should help you get under way.

Keep in mind that although *the following exercises are relative to the Key of C Major,* the **CHORD FORMULA** remains the same for **ANY MAJOR KEY** . . . based on the **MAJOR SCALE PATTERN**.

THE I CHORD (TONIC)

MAJOR TRIAD BUILT ON THE 1-3-5 NOTES OF THE MAJOR SCALE

Key of C Major

PLAY WITH SEPARATE HANDS, AT FIRST
. . . THEN WITH BOTH HANDS TOGETHER

REPEAT EACH EXERCISE 4 TIMES
(IN TEMPO)

C MAJOR TRIAD

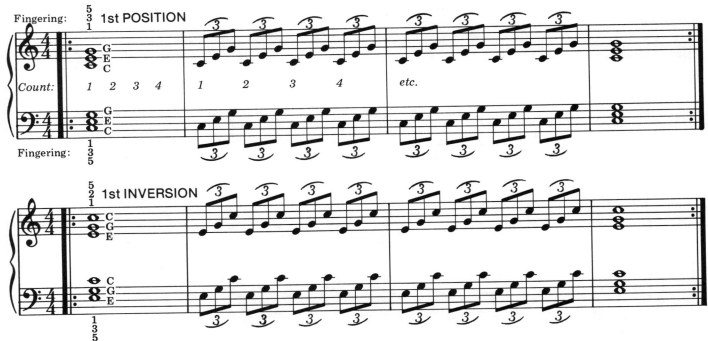

A **CHORD** has as many **INVERSIONS** as it has notes above the **KEY NOTE**.

THE MAJOR TRIAD, A THREE-PART CHORD, HAS *TWO* **INVERSIONS.**

C MAJOR TRIAD

THE IV CHORD (SUB-DOMINANT)

The Major Triad built *from* the *4th* or Sub-Dominant note of the Major Scale. Notes of 1 - 3 - 5 of the Major Scale of the Key starting on the Dominant note.

In the Key of C Major the *4th* note is F. The Major Triad built from *that* note would be F - A - C or notes 1 - 3 - 5 of the new Key of F Major.

RELATIVE TO THE KEY OF C MAJOR

PLAY WITH SEPARATE HANDS, AT FIRST
... THEN WITH BOTH HANDS TOGETHER

REPEAT EACH EXERCISE 4 TIMES, IN TEMPO

F MAJOR TRIAD

NOTE . . . the *IV CHORD OF THE KEY OF C MAJOR* is the **SAME CHORD** as the *I CHORD OF THE KEY OF F MAJOR.*

110

F MAJOR TRIAD

2nd INVERSION

Play as in key of F major

THE V CHORD (DOMINANT)

The Major Triad built *from* the *5th* of Dominant note of the Major Scale. Notes of 1 - 3 - 5 of the Major Scale of the Key starting on the Dominant note.

In the Key of C Major the *5th* note is G. The Major triad built from *that* note would be G - B - D or notes 1 - 3 - 5 of the new Key of G Major.

RELATIVE TO THE KEY OF C MAJOR

PLAY WITH SEPARATE HANDS, AT FIRST
...THEN WITH BOTH HANDS TOGETHER

REPEAT EACH EXERCISE 4 TIMES, IN TEMPO

G MAJOR TRIAD

1st POSITION

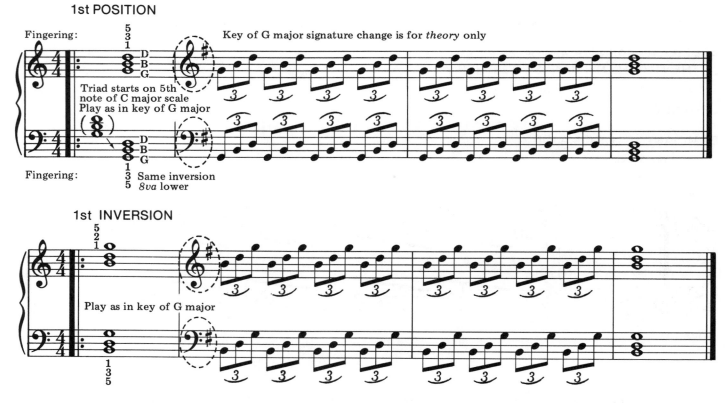

Fingering:

Key of G major signature change is for *theory* only

Triad starts on 5th note of C major scale
Play as in key of G major

Fingering: Same inversion *8va* lower

1st INVERSION

Play as in key of G major

NOTE... the *V CHORD OF THE KEY OF C MAJOR* is the **SAME CHORD** as the *I CHORD OF THE KEY OF G MAJOR*.

G MAJOR TRIAD

2nd INVERSION

THE V7 CHORD (DOMINANT SEVENTH)

This Chord is based on the *5th* note or **DOMINANT** note of the Major Scale. To the **DOMINANT MAJOR TRIAD** (1 - 3 - 5 notes of the Key starting on the Dominant note) **ADD** the note **THREE HALF STEPS** above. This is the "Flatted Seventh" note (♭7) of the **NEW KEY.**

In the Exercise below you will notice . . . *in the Key of C Major* the Dominant Triad is G - B - D, or the Major Triad of this **NEW KEY** of G Major. The 7th note of the G Major Scale being F♯, we lower or "flat" this note ½ step to make the "Flatted Seventh," then **ADD** this note to the G Major Triad . . . thus we have the complete **DOMINANT SEVENTH CHORD** of C Major, or notes G - B - D - F♮ .

RELATIVE TO THE KEY OF C MAJOR

REPEAT EACH EXERCISE 4 TIMES, IN TEMPO

PLAY WITH SEPARATE HANDS, AT FIRST
. . . THEN WITH BOTH HANDS TOGETHER

G7TH CHORD

DOMINANT 7TH OF C MAJOR

1st POSITION

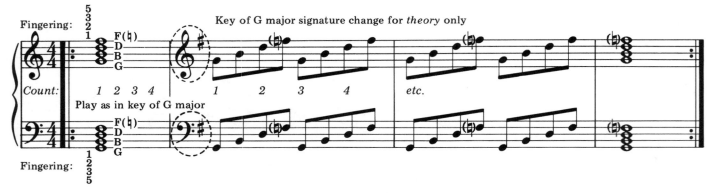

THE DOMINANT 7TH CHORD, A FOUR-PART CHORD, HAS *THREE* INVERSIONS.

G7th CHORD
DOMINANT 7TH OF C MAJOR

1st INVERSION

Play as in key of G major

2nd INVERSION

Play as in key of G major

3rd INVERSION

Same inversion
8va lower
Play as in key of G major

FOR AN EXCELLENT STUDY EXERCISE . . . Figure out the *I, IV, V & V7 CHORDS* of the Major Keys of F, G, B♭, D, E♭ and A, and **PLAY THEM, TOGETHER WITH THE INVERSIONS, AS CHORD-FINGER EXERCISES . . .** *as you did the above for the Key of C Major.*

NEXT . . . We shall try **"FEELING THE** *MINOR* **KEY CHORDS."**

FEELING THE CHORDS

— MINOR KEY CHORDS WITH INVERSIONS —

A CHORD EXERCISE

Like the **MAJOR KEYS**, the **MINOR KEYS** have their own *I, IV* and *V CHORD FORMULA,* as explained in the **MINOR KEY** section, previously. While the exercises below are in the *Key of A Minor (the Relative Minor of the Key of C Major),* the **MINOR CHORD FORMULA WOULD REMAIN THE SAME IN** *ANY* **MINOR KEY . . .** based on the **MINOR SCALE.**

first, let's play the *CHORDS* in sequence, and in tempo, as a *CHORD EXERCISE.*

PLAY WITH SEPARATE HANDS, AT FIRST
. . . THEN WITH BOTH HANDS TOGETHER

REPEAT EACH EXERCISE 4 TIMES

Key of A Minor (Relative to Key of C Major)

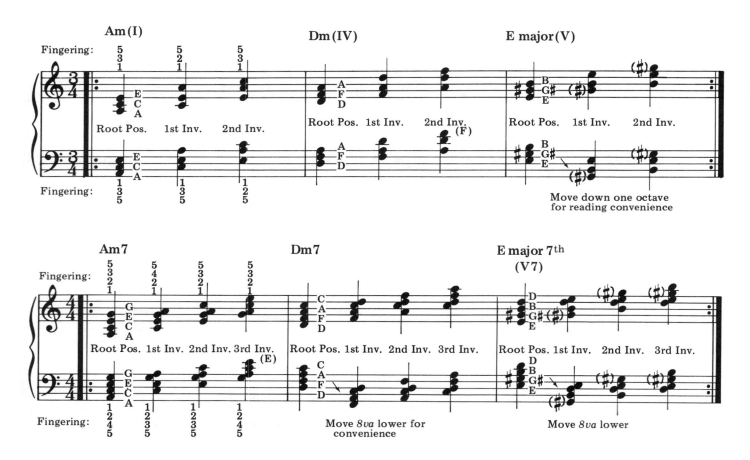

You have played the **I, IV** and **V MINOR KEY CHORDS,** plus the **added SEVENTH CHORDS** . . . A Minor 7th, D Minor 7th and the E Major 7th - same as the V7 Chord.

NOW . . . we shall break down the **MINOR KEY CHORDS** into *FINGER EXERCISES* to get the real *FEELING OF THE CHORDS:*

114

FEELING THE CHORDS

— MINOR KEY CHORDS · 1ST POSITION —

CHORD · FINGER EXERCISES

PLAY SEPARATE HANDS, AT FIRST
. . . THEN BOTH HANDS TOGETHER

REPEAT THIS EIGHT MEASURE
EXERCISE 3 TIMES, IN TEMPO

Key of A Minor (Relative Minor of C Major)

Fingering: *r.h.* 1-3-5
l.h. 5-3-1

THE I CHORD

THE IV CHORD

THE V CHORD

THE I CHORD (8va Higher)

Repeat

THE MINOR KEY *SEVENTH* CHORDS

SEPARATE HANDS, AT FIRST
. . . THEN BOTH HANDS TOGETHER

REPEAT 3 TIMES, IN TEMPO

EXERCISE: Figure out the Relative Minor Keys for the Major Keys of F, G, B♭, D, E♭ and A . . . **THEN** work out the **I, IV** and **V CHORDS,** plus the **added SEVENTHS,** for each respective **MINOR KEY.**

Play the **CHORDS,** then the **FINGER EXERCISES** in the same fashion as the study above.

Remember, when planning a Minor *Scale* Pattern, it is based on the Key Signature of the relative Major Key. This is important in determining the location of the I, IV and V degrees of a particular Minor Scale.

116

A LOOK AHEAD WITH NEW, RICH SOUNDING CHORDS...
FULL CHORDS SUPPORTING A POPULAR STYLED MELODY

NEW SOUND IN TOWN

By MATT DENNIS a.s.c.a.p.

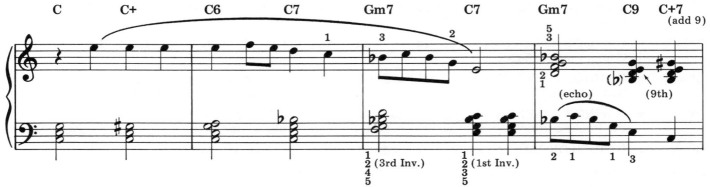

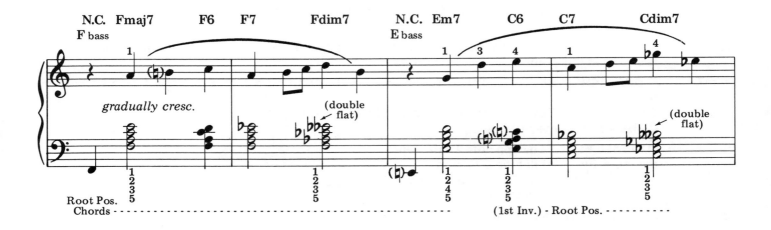

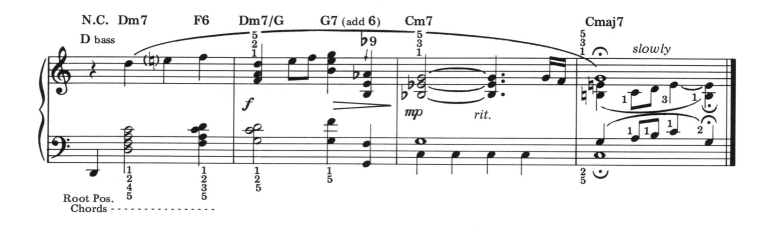

FORMATION OF THE CHORDS USED IN ABOVE SELECTION . . . The following rules may be applied to Chords based on the Major Scale Pattern of **ANY KEY-ROOT POSITIONS GIVEN:**

C = C **MAJOR TRIAD.** 1-3-5 notes of the Major Scale Pattern. The I Chord.

C+ = C **AUGMENTED CHORD.** 5th note of the Major Scale (3rd note of the Major Triad) is **raised** or **sharped** ½ step. Play notes 1-3- ♯5.

C6 = C **SIXTH CHORD.** 6th note of the Major Scale is **added** to the Major Triad. The 6th may also be added to the 7th or 9th Chords of **ANY KEY.**

C7 = C **SEVENTH CHORD.** To the Major Triad **add** the note 3 half steps above. Known as the **V7** Chord. In Key of C Major play C-E-G-B♭.

Cmaj7 = C **MAJOR SEVENTH CHORD.** To the Major Triad **add** the 7th note of the Major Scale. In Key of C Major play C-E-G-B.

Cmaj9 = C **MAJOR NINTH CHORD.** Simply **add** the 9th note (a whole step above the 8th note of the Major Scale) to the Major 7th Chord, as an **extension.** In Key of C Major notes read C-E-G-B-D.

Gm7 = G **MINOR SEVENTH CHORD.** See definition of Minor 7th Chords in previous study. In Key of G the Root Position Chord would read G-B♭-D-F. In above piece the Chord is played in the 3rd Inversion.

C9 = C **NINTH CHORD.** To the 7th (V7) Chord **add** the 9th note. An **extension** of the 7th Chord.

(add 9) = **ADDED NINTH NOTE.** The 9th note may be **added** to the 6th, Major 7th or V7 Chords as an **extension,** for a full modern sound.

C+7(add 9) = C **AUGMENTED SEVENTH CHORD WITH ADDED NINTH. Sharp** the 5th ½ step, **add** the 9th note to the 7th Chord. In Key of C Major notes read C-E-G♯-B♭-D. Best played when "voiced" between hands, as shown.

NC = **NO CHORD.** Just a single bass note is indicated by the "F Bass" in above piece. No **harmony** is shown at this point.

Fdim7 = F **DIMINISHED SEVENTH CHORD.** The regular 7th (V7) Chord becomes a **diminished** Chord by **flatting** or lowering the 3rd, 5th and 7th notes ½ step each, keeping the Root or Key Note intact. Example: F7th: F-A-C-E♭; **Fdim7: F-A♭-C♭-E♭♭** (double flat). E♭♭ becomes same note as D♮. . . C♭ becomes same note as B♮.

♭♭ = "DOUBLE FLAT." **Lower** a note **2 half steps.**
Example: E♭. . just flat the E ½ step;
E♭♭. . . flat the E 2 half steps or 1 whole step. . .
The note becomes same as D♮.

♭9 = **FLATTED NINTH NOTE.** Simply **flat** the 9th note ½ step.

PLAY OVER THE ABOVE SELECTION SEVERAL TIMES, and study these new Popular Chords, working them out in various Keys according to the fundamental rules above. Become familiar with these Contemporary Sounds, as you will be experiencing such Chords in future studies and Popular music you may play.

ANOTHER ADVENTURE WITH CONTEMPORARY CHORDS

LITTLE JAZZ

By MATT DENNIS a.s.c.a.p.

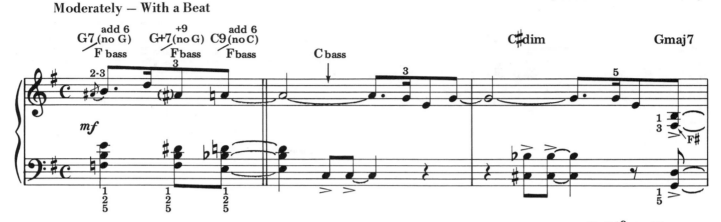

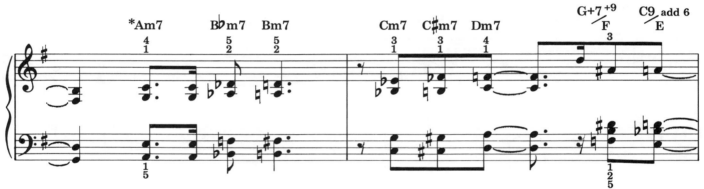

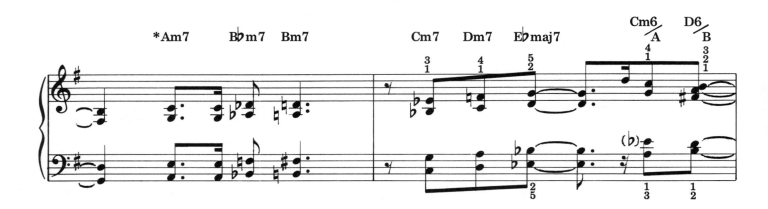

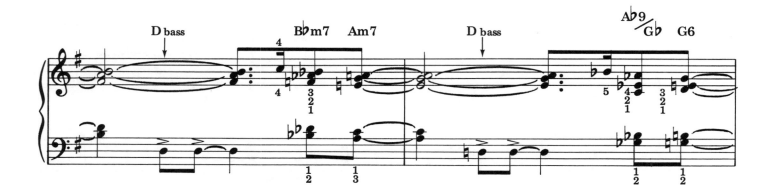

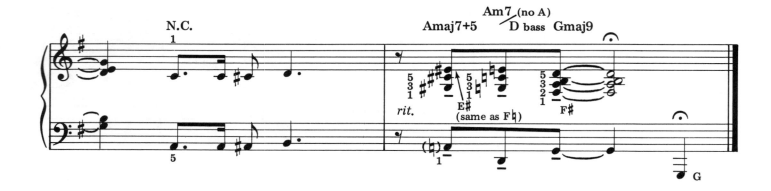

CHORD SYMBOL EXPLANATIONS for chords used in **LITTLE JAZZ.**
The Chords used above are shown in various "voiced" Positions or Inversions. An indicated "bass" note will usually determine a basic Position or Inversion of a Chord.

G7(no G) add 6 / F bass
= G7th Chord with added 6th (E), and an F bass note. The **G** is left out in the "voicing" of the Inversion of this Chord.

G+7(no G) +9 / F bass
= G7th Chord with Augmented or sharped 5th (D$\sharp$), plus a sharped or raised 9th (A$\sharp$), with an F bass note. The **G** is left out, as explained above.

C9 add 6 / E bass
= C9th Chord with added 6th (A), and an E bass note. The **C** is left out in the "voicing" of this Chord.

C$\sharp$ dim
= C$\sharp$ Diminished 7th Chord. Enough essential notes are given to establish identity of this Chord. (C$\sharp$, E, G, B$\flat$). See previous rule for the Diminished 7th Chord.

*
= **NOTE** the interesting series of Minor 7th Chords, as smoothly played in **rising chromatic half steps** (Am7, B$\flat$m7, Bm7, Cm7, C$\sharp$m7, Dm7).

N.C.
= **N**o Chord at this point. Single notes are played.

Dm7 addG
= Dm7th Chord with added note of G.

D6 / B bass
= D6th Chord with a B bass note.

A$\flat$9 / G$\flat$ bass
= A$\flat$9th Chord with a G$\flat$ bass note. This Chord is so "voiced" that the 7th and 9th notes are played by the L.H. in the bass clef, for a rich sound.

Amaj7 +5
= A Major 7th Chord with added Augmented or sharped 5th (E$\sharp$). Remember, E$\sharp$ is the same sounding note as F$\natural$. A Close-harmony Chord, leading nicely to the Am7/D bass and G Major 9th Chords.

Am7 (no A) / D bass
= A Minor 7th Chord with a D bass note. A full sounding Chord resolving naturally to the final G Major 9th Chord. The **A** is left out in the special "voicing" of this Chord.

SHORT MUSICAL DICTIONARY

The following terms and signs are used throughout **You Can Teach Yourself Piano**. They are some of the most popularly used expressions in music; and by observing them you are able to add dynamics, style, and tonal color to the music you play.

General Terms

CODA ⊕ .... Play from this sign to end of piece

D.C. (Da Capo) .... Return to beginning and repeat

* D.C. al Coda .... Return to beginning, play to words "To Coda ⊕ " — go to **CODA** ⊕ and play out

D.C. al Fine.............................. Return to beginning and play to "Fine"

* D.S. al Coda .... Return to this sign 𝄋 then to words "To Coda ⊕ " — go to **CODA** ⊕ and play out.

Fermata ⌢ .... Hold note longer than written, pause

To Coda ⊕ .... Go directly to **CODA** ⊕ and play out

Tempo, Rhythm

Allegro.................................. Lively, joyful, cheerful

Andante................................. Moderately slow

Moderato (Moderately) .... Medium or moderate speed

rit. (Ritardando) .... Gradually slower

Tempo .... Speed of a study or piece

Tempo di Marcia .... Play as a March

Tempo di Valse .... Play as a Waltz (3/4 time)

Dynamics, Volume

Accent (>) .... Emphasize, play louder

cresc. (Crescendo) ⎯⎯⎯⎯ .... Gradually play louder

dim. (Diminuendo) ⎯⎯⎯⎯ .... Gradually play softer

f (forte) .... Loud

mf (mezzo forte)........................ Medium loud

mp (mezzo piano)....................... Medium soft

p (piano)............................... Soft

Expression, Feeling

Legato .... Smoothly, connected

Staccato .... Short, disconnected

Miscellaneous

Repeat sign 𝄇 .... Go back to beginning and play again

C (Common Time)....................... Same as 4/4 time

Books in the "You Can Teach Yourself" Series

You Can Teach Yourself About Music
by L. Dean Bye

You Can Teach Yourself Dulcimer
by Madeline MacNeil

You Can Teach Yourself Electric Bass
by Mike Hiland

You Can Teach Yourself Guitar
by William Bay

You Can Teach Yourself Harmonica
by George Heaps-Nelson & Barbara McClintock Koehler

You Can Teach Yourself Piano
by Matt Dennis

You Can Teach Yourself Piano by Ear
by Robin Jarman

You Can Teach Yourself Recorder
&
You Can Teach Yourself Recorder Book/Recorder Package
by William Bay

You Can Teach Yourself Rock Guitar
by Vince Lauria & Mark Lonergan

Great Music at Your Fingertips